Sculthorp

• HBJ READING PROGRAM •

WEATHER VANES

➤➤➤ LAUREATE EDITION ◀◀◀

LEVEL 6

Bernice E. Cullinan
Roger C. Farr
W. Dorsey Hammond
Nancy L. Roser
Dorothy S. Strickland

8468

HBJ **HARCOURT BRACE JOVANOVICH, PUBLISHERS**
Orlando   San Diego   Chicago   Dallas

Acknowledgments

For permission to reprint copyrighted material, grateful acknowledgment is made to the following sources:

Curtis Brown, Ltd.: Adapted from *The Simple Prince* by Jane Yolen. Copyright © 1978 by Jane Yolen. Published by Parents' Magazine Press.

Carolrhoda Books, Inc., 241 First Avenue North, Minneapolis, MN 55401: From *Cornstalks and Cannonballs* by Barbara Mitchell. Copyright © 1980 by Carolrhoda Books, Inc.

Coward, McCann & Geoghegan: Adapted from *Forecast* by Malcolm Hall. Text copyright © 1977 by Malcolm Hall.

E. P. Dutton, a division of NAL Penguin Inc.: Adapted from *Clyde Monster* by Robert L. Crowe, illustrated by Kay Chorao. Text copyright © 1976 by Robert L. Crowe; illustrations copyright © 1976 by Kay Sproat Chorao.

E. P. Dutton, a division of NAL Penguin Inc. and The Canadian Publishers, McClelland and Stewart Limited, Toronto: "Politeness" from *When We Were Very Young* by A. A. Milne. Copyright 1924 by E. P. Dutton, renewed 1952 by A. A. Milne.

Greenwillow Books, a division of William Morrow & Company, Inc.: "Night is Here" from *My Parents Think I'm Sleeping* by Jack Prelutsky. Text copyright © 1985 by Jack Prelutsky. Abridged and adapted from *Jenny and the Tennis Nut* by Janet Schulman. Copyright © 1978 by Janet Schulman.

Harcourt Brace Jovanovich, Inc.: Abridged and adapted from *Jane Martin, Dog Detective* by Eve Bunting. Copyright © 1984 by Eve Bunting. Abridged and adapted text from *Sun Up, Sun Down* by Gail Gibbons. Copyright © 1983 by Gail Gibbons.

Harper & Row, Publishers, Inc.: Complete text, abridged and adapted, and illustrations from *Arthur's Honey Bear* by Lillian Hoban. Copyright © 1974 by Lillian Hoban. Complete text, abridged and adapted, and illustrations from *Barkley*, written and illustrated by Syd Hoff. Copyright © 1975 by Syd Hoff. Text and illustrations from "Owl and the Moon" in *Owl at Home*, written and illustrated by Arnold Lobel. Copyright © 1975 by Arnold Lobel.

Henry Holt and Company, Inc.: "Keepsakes" from *Is Somewhere Always Far Away?* by Leland B. Jacobs. Copyright © 1967 by Leland B. Jacobs.

Jane W. Krows: "The New Year" by Jane W. Krows.

G. P. Putnam's Sons: "Everybody Says" from *Everything and Anything* by Dorothy Aldis. Copyright 1925-27, renewed 1953-55 by Dorothy Aldis. Adapted from *The Quilt Story* by Tony Johnston, illustrated by Tomie dePaola. Text © 1985 by Tony Johnston; illustrations © 1985 by Tomie dePaola.

Marian Reiner on behalf of Myra Cohn Livingston: "My Dog" from *The Moon and a Star and Other Poems* by Myra Cohn Livingston. Copyright © 1965 by Myra Cohn Livingston.

Charles Scribner's Sons, a division of Macmillan, Inc.: Adapted from *How the Sun Made a Promise and Kept It* by Margery Bernstein and Janet Kobrin. Copyright © 1974, 1972 by Margery Bernstein and Janet Kobrin.

Martha Shapp: Adapted from *Let's Find Out About New Year's Day* (Retitled: "New Year's Day") by Martha and Charles Shapp. Published by Franklin Watts, Inc., 1968.

Karen S. Solomon: "Change in the Weather" by Ilo Orleans.

Viking Penguin Inc.: Adapted from *Watch Out, Ronald Morgan!* by Patricia Reilly Giff. Copyright © 1985 by Patricia Reilly Giff.

Franklin Watts, Inc.: From *Beatrice Doesn't Want To* by Laura Joffe Numeroff. Text copyright © 1981 by Laura Joffe Numeroff.

Albert Whitman & Company: From *Nick Joins In*, written and illustrated by Joe Lasker. Copyright © 1984 by Joe Lasker. From *Grandma Without Me*, story and pictures by Judith Vigna. Copyright © 1984 by Judith Vigna.

Key: (l)–Left; (r)–Right; (c)–Center; (t)–Top; (b)–Bottom

Photographs

Page iii, Ed Cooper; iv P. Kresan/H. Armstrong Roberts; vi Comstock; vii, HBJ Photo/John Petrey; 2, Ed Cooper; 58 (l), HBJ Photo/Richard Stacks, Courtesy of the San Fransico S.P.C.A. Hearing Dog Program; 58 (r), HBJ Photo/Richard Stacks, Courtesy of Guide Dogs For The Blind, San Rafael; 59 (all), HBJ Photo/Richard Stacks; 60 (both), HBJ Photo/Richard Stacks; 61, HBJ Photo/Richard Stacks; 62, HBJ Photo/Richard Stacks; 65, Ed Cooper; 66, Colour Library International; 67, P. Kresan/H. Armstrong Roberts; 130 (tl), Joel Gordon; 130 (lc), Comstock; 130 (bl), Joel Gordon; 130 (c), Joel Gordon; 130 (tr), Joel Gordon; 130 (rc), Joel Gordon; 130 (br), Joel Gordon; 186 (l), M. Fogden/Bruce Coleman, Inc.; 186 (r), J.H. Robinson/Photo Researchers; 187 (tl), M. Williams/Photo Nats; 187 (bl) D. Overcash/Bruce Coleman, Inc.; 187 (tr), L. Stone/Bruce Coleman, Inc; 187 (br), J. & D. Bartlett/Bruce Coleman, Inc.; 188 (l), E.R. Degginger; 186 (r), National Audubon Society/Photo Researchers; 189, M. Williams/Photo Nats; 190, E.R. Degginger; 197, HBJ Photo; 198–199, HBJ Photo/John Petrey; 214, HBJ Photo/Jerry White; 215, HBJ Photo/Jerry White; 216, HBJ Photo/Jerry White; 217, HBJ Photo/Jerry White; 218, HBJ Photo/Jerry White; 275, HBJ Photo/John Petrey

Illustrators

Lynn Uhde Adams: 192–195; Cheryl Arnemann: 82–86; Robert Baumgartner: 118–126; Dave Blanchette: 210–211; Alex Block: 6–12, 80; Eulala Conner: 134–142, 144, 204; Carolyn Croll: 178–184, 213; Virginia Curtain: 236–237; John Cymerman: 78–79; Helen K. Davie: 100–101; Jim Deigan: 106–110; Tommie dePaola: 252–258; Lilian Hoban: 260–272; Syd Hoff: 48–54; Pam Johnson: 146–150; Eric Joyner: 166–174; Joe Lasker: 20–28; Dora Leder: 30–31; Bruce Lemerise: 4–5, 68–69, 132–133, 200–201; Arnold Lobel: 112–116; Mary MacLaren: 279–301; Diana Magnuson: 230–234; Mike Muir: 220–228, 238; Jim Moble: 154–155; Dan Siculan: 14–18, 240–250; Blanche Sims: 34–44; Joe Veno: 88–98; Judith Vigna: 202–208; Justin Wager: 152–162; Lane Yerkes: 56–57, 176–177.
Cover: Kinuko Craft

HBJ Maps and Charts pp. 103, 105

Contents

Unit 1
Stepping Stones 2

Read on Your Own 4

Watch Out, Ronald Morgan! 6
by Patricia Reilly Giff (Realistic Fiction)
from WATCH OUT, RONALD MORGAN!

Benjamin Franklin's Glasses 14
by Sally McMillan (Biography)

Nick Joins In 20
story and pictures by Joe Lasker
(Realistic Fiction)
from NICK JOINS IN

Someone 30
by Carol Quinn (Poem)

Draw Conclusions 32
(Comprehension Study)

Jane Martin, Dog Detective 34
by Eve Bunting (Mystery)
from JANE MARTIN, DOG DETECTIVE

Reality and Fantasy 46
(Literature Study)

Barkley 48
story and pictures by Syd Hoff (Fantasy)
from BARKLEY

My Dog 56
by Myra Cohn Livingston (Poem)
from THE MOON AND A STAR AND
OTHER POEMS

Dogs at Work 58
by Phyllis Hoffman (Informational Article)

Thinking About "Stepping Stones" 64

Unit 2
Earth and Sky 66

Read on Your Own 68

Clyde Monster 70
by Robert L. Crowe (Fantasy)
from CLYDE MONSTER

Night is Here 78
  by Jack Prelutsky   (Poem)
  from MY PARENTS THINK I'M SLEEPING

Cause and Effect 80
  (Comprehension Study)

Sun Up, Sun Down 82
  by Gail Gibbons
  (Informational Article)
  from SUN UP, SUN DOWN

Forecast 88
  by Malcolm Hall   (Fantasy)
  from FORECAST

Change in the Weather 100
  by Ilo Orleans   (Poem)

Maps 102
  (Study Skills)

Splash 106
  by Ronda Maseman
  (Informational Article)

Owl and the Moon 112
  story and pictures by Arnold Lobel
  (Fantasy)
  from OWL AT HOME

v

**How the Sun Made a Promise
and Kept It** 118
retold by Margery Bernstein and Janet Kobrin
(A Canadian Indian Myth)
from HOW THE SUN MADE A PROMISE
AND KEPT IT

Thinking About "Earth and Sky" 128

Unit 3
Kaleidoscopes 130

Read on Your Own 132

Beatrice Doesn't Want To 134
by Laura Joffe Numeroff   (Realistic Fiction)
from BEATRICE DOESN'T WANT TO

Main Idea and Details 144
(Comprehension Study)

Tell Me a Story 146
by Donald Cooper   (Informational Article)

The Simple Prince 152
by Jane Yolen   (Realistic Fiction)
from THE SIMPLE PRINCE

Politeness 164
by A. A. Milne
from WHEN WE WERE VERY YOUNG

Jenny and the Tennis Nut 166
  by Janet Schulman (Realistic Fiction)
  from JENNY AND THE TENNIS NUT

Everybody Says 176
  by Dorothy Aldis (Poem)
  from HERE, THERE & EVERYWHERE

The Ugly Duckling 178
  A fairy tale retold by Frank Ruggiero
  (Play)

The Caterpillar's Surprise 186
  by Grace Moremen
  (Informational Article)

Follow Directions 192
  (Study Skills)

Thinking About "Kaleidoscopes" 196

Unit 4
Scrapbooks

Scrapbooks 198

Read on Your Own 200

Grandma Without Me 202
  story and pictures by Judith Vigna
  (Realistic Fiction)
  from GRANDMA WITHOUT ME

Keepsakes 210
by *Leland B. Jacobs*   (Poem)
from IS SOMEWHERE ALWAYS FAR AWAY?

Summarize 212
(Comprehension Study)

Scrapbooks 214
by *Alma Marshak Whitney*
(Informational Article)

The Year of the Smile 220
by *John Yeates*   (Realistic Fiction)

New Year's Day 230
by *Martha and Charles Shapp*
(Informational Article)
from LET'S FIND OUT ABOUT
NEW YEAR'S DAY

The New Year 236
by *Jane W. Krows*   (Poem)

Story Elements 238
(Literature Study)

Cornstalks and Cannonballs 240
by *Barbara Mitchell*   (Legend)
from CORNSTALKS AND CANNONBALLS

The Quilt Story 252
by *Tony Johnston*   (Realistic Fiction)
from THE QUILT STORY

Bonus: Arthur's Honey Bear 260
story and pictures by Lillian Hoban   (Fantasy)
from ARTHUR'S HONEY BEAR

Thinking About "Scrapbooks" 274

Glossary 276

Word List 303

Awards

The authors and illustrators of selections in this book have received the following awards either for their work in this book or for another of their works. The specific award is indicated under the medallion on the opening page of each award-winning selection.

American Library Association Notable
  Children's Books
Best work of fiction from the California Council
Randolph Caldecott Medal
Randolph Caldecott Honor Award
Lewis Carroll Shelf Award
Children's Choices
Christopher Award
Commonwealth Club of California
Garden State Children's Book Award
Golden Kite Award
Junior Literary Guild Selection
National Book Award
National Council of Teachers of English Award for Excellence
  in Poetry
John Newbery Honor Award
John Newbery Medal
New York Times Best Illustrated Children's Books
  of the Year
New York Times Outstanding Books
NSTA–CBC Outstanding Science Trade Book for Children
School Library Journal Best Book
Southern California Council on Literature for Children
  and Young People Awards

Unit 1

Stepping Stones

In "Stepping Stones," you will read about people and animals who are doing something new. Some may be trying something for the very first time. Others may be looking at old things in new ways. Others may be making new friends.

As you read "Stepping Stones," think about how the people and animals in each story take a step to make friends or to look at things in new ways. See how they learn by taking things one step at a time. See what fun it can be to try something new!

Read on Your Own

Bunnies and Their Sports *by Nancy Carlson. Viking.* This is a short, funny story telling about healthy bunnies.

Loudmouth George and the Neighbors *by Nancy Carlson. Carolrhoda Bks.* George does not want to meet his new neighbors because they are pigs and not bunnies.

Good As New *by Barbara Douglass. Lothrop.* Even Grandpa cannot make Grady's spoiled little cousin K.C. happy.

Lionel at Large *by Stephen Krensky. Dial.* Lionel overcomes problems such as eating vegetables, going to a doctor, and looking for a lost snake.

Amy Goes Fishing *by Jean Marzollo. Dial.*
Amy discovers that fishing is not boring
when she spends the day with her
father.

The Happy Birthday Mystery *by Joan Lowery
Nixon. Whitman.* What happens to the
birthday surprise that Mike and Susan
bring Mrs. Pickett?

Big Max *by Kin Platt. Harper.* The world's
greatest detective helps the King of Pooka
find his prize elephant.

Libby's New Glasses *by Tricia Tusa. Holiday.*
Libby does not like her new glasses until
she meets an ostrich who hides its head
in the sand to hide its new glasses. Then
she changes her mind.

Ronald Morgan needs glasses. He thinks that the glasses will make him a superkid. What does Ronald find out?

Watch Out, Ronald Morgan!

by Patricia Reilly Giff

It all started when I raced across the school yard and slid on a patch of ice.

"Watch out!" Rosemary yelled. But it was too late. I bumped into her, and she landed in a snow pile.

After I hung up my coat, I fed the goldfish. I fed Frank, the gerbil, too.

"Oh, no," Rosemary said. "You fed the gerbil food to Goldie!"

"The boxes look the same," I said.

Billy shook his head. "Can't you read the letters? *F* is for fish. *G* is for gerbil."

"It's all right," said my friend Michael. He put more water into the fish tank.

After lunch we looked outside. Everything was white. "It's time for a winter classroom," said Miss Tyler. I sat down and drew a snowflake. Then I cut it out.

Tom said, "Ronald Morgan, that's a funny snowflake. Why don't you cut on the lines?"

When it was time to go, Miss Tyler gave me a note to take home. "Maybe you need glasses," she said.

At lunch the next day, Marc asked, "When do you get your glasses?"

"I go to Doctor Sims's office today," I answered.

Michael asked, "Can I go with you?"

When we got to Doctor Sims's office, Doctor Sims said, "Look at these *E*'s. Which way do they point?" I pointed. Then the *E*'s looked smaller and smaller. Doctor Sims said, "It's hard for you to see them."

My mother said, "You'll look great in glasses."

"Yes," said Doctor Sims. "Glasses will help. They'll make everything look sharp and clear."

I tried on red frames. They slid down over my nose. Then I put on blue frames.

"Good," said my mother.

"Good," said Michael.

Then Doctor Sims said, "The glasses will be ready in a little while."

When my glasses were ready, I said, "I'll be the superkid of the school."

Before school, I threw some snowballs. "You missed!" Jimmy yelled.

Michael said, "How come your glasses don't work?"

In the classroom, I hung up my coat and put my hat away.

"Where is our fish person?" asked Miss Tyler.

I ran to give Goldie some food. This time I looked at the box. The letters looked big and sharp. "G is for Goldie," I said. "F is for Frank."

"Oh, no," said Billy. "F is for fish. G is for gerbil."

Michael said, "I don't think your glasses help."

I put the glasses inside my hat.

Alice looked at me. "Why aren't you wearing your blue glasses?" she asked.

I shook my head. "My glasses don't work. I'll never be the superkid of the class."

When it was time to go home, Miss Tyler gave me another note. My mother helped me with some of the words.

I know you are sad about your glasses. Glasses will not make you throw better. You have to keep throwing a ball again and again. Also, you'll still trip if you don't watch out. Glasses help you see better. They make everything sharp and clear. Please wear your glasses.   Love, Miss Tyler

P.S. You ARE a superkid.

In school the next day, I drew a snowman and cut it out. "Hey," I said, "Miss Tyler's right. The lines are sharp and clear."

"Good snowman," said Rosemary.

Miss Tyler said, "Just what we need for our winter classroom."

I drew blue glasses on my snowman. "Now he's a super snowman," I said. We all clapped.

1. What does Ronald find out about his glasses?

2. Why did Ronald draw glasses on his snowman?

3. How did Miss Tyler help Ronald get used to his new glasses?

4. How did you feel when you read, "I'll be the superkid of the school "?

5. When did you first begin to think that Ronald's glasses weren't going to solve his problems?

**Think
and
Write**

Think about what makes someone a superkid. Write a paragraph that tells four things that would make a kid a superkid.

Benjamin Franklin discovered many things that are still used by people today. How did Benjamin Franklin help some people see better?

Benjamin Franklin's Glasses

by Sally McMillan

Benjamin Franklin did many things. He was a printer. He discovered electricity. He also liked to write books and newspapers. He even helped to write some of the first laws for the United States.

Benjamin stopped going to school when he was only ten years old. He had to go to work. Benjamin still wanted to learn, even if he was not in school. He learned many things just by reading. He was always reading. He read anything he could find.

Benjamin Franklin was always coming up with new ideas. One of his ideas was the Franklin stove. He made a stove that stood inside a fireplace. It made a room much hotter than a fireplace did. Even today, people use stoves that are very much like the stove that Franklin made.

As Franklin grew older, he found he needed glasses. He needed one pair of glasses to see things that were near. He needed another pair of glasses to see things that were far away.

"I want to read books. I want to look at fire, water, and the stars. I don't want two pairs of glasses. I want just one pair so that I can see both near and far away," he said.

So Franklin took the top part of his glasses for faraway things. He took the bottom part of his glasses for near things. Then Franklin put them together and made one new pair of glasses.

Franklin put on the glasses.

"This is what I need," he said.

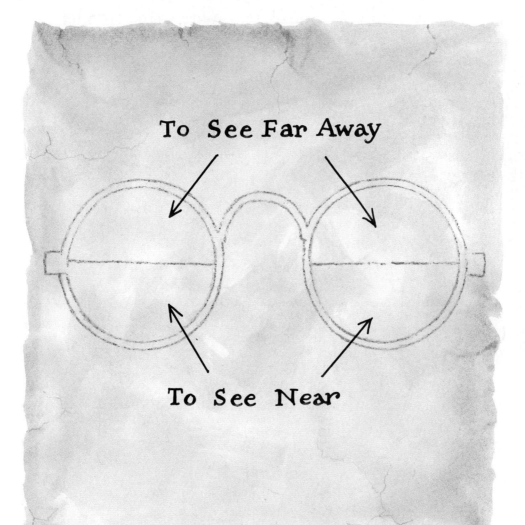

To See Far Away

To See Near

"When I look up, I can see things that are far away. When I look down, I can see things that are near. I think I will call my new glasses bifocals." With his new glasses Franklin kept on reading and learning.

Benjamin Franklin made bifocals so that people needed only one pair of glasses to see both near and far away. The bifocals that people wear today are very much like the ones Franklin made many years ago.

1. How did Benjamin Franklin help some people see better?

2. What kind of glasses did Benjamin Franklin make?

3. Was Franklin's idea to make bifocals a good one? Why?

4. What part of the story made you think that Benjamin Franklin would make bifocal glasses?

Think about Benjamin Franklin's inventions. Which one of his inventions do you think is most important? Write a thank-you note to Benjamin telling him how the invention has helped people.

Nick is going to school with other children for the first time. What does Nick think of the school and the new friends he meets there?

Nick Joins In

story and pictures by Joe Lasker

Nick was afraid. Soon he would be going to school. No longer would a teacher come to his home.

Nick talked to his parents. "How can I go to school in my wheelchair?" he asked. "What if the kids don't like me? Will there be anyone else in the school who can't walk?"

20

On and on, Nick's questions spilled out. "We know why you feel so afraid," his parents said. Nick felt a little better.

On Wednesday morning a small yellow bus took Nick to his school. A teacher met the bus. "We hope you like our school, Nick," she said. The teacher pushed Nick down a long hall and into his new classroom.

Everyone in the room looked at Nick. His teacher, Mrs. Becker, smiled at him. "We're glad you're here," she said. Then she told Nick the names of the boys and girls in the class.

No one spoke. Then Mrs. Becker said, "Nick, I think the children would like to ask you some questions. Is that all right?" Nick nodded, looking down.

Rachel asked the first question.

"Why do you have to use a wheelchair?"

"Because I can't walk," Nick said.

"Why can't you walk?" asked Nina.

"Because my legs didn't grow right."

"Why is that?" asked Timmie.

Nick looked at him. "I've always been this way."

Then Mrs. Becker said, "All right, boys and girls, it's time to get back to work." Then she helped Nick get started.

Nick looked at all the children, at his teacher, and at the bright pictures on the walls. He didn't feel so afraid anymore. He felt he might like this school.

Days went by. Nick and the other children grew used to each other. They learned from one another.

Without being asked, people helped Nick. He helped people, too. Sometimes Nick helped the gym teacher open windows with the long window pole.

Nick made friends. One of them was
Timmie. Nick loved to go outside with
the other children.

For the first time in his life, Nick
played outdoor games. He couldn't run
like Timmie, but he moved fast.

What Nick wished for most was to play
ball like the others. How fast and high
they ran and jumped! To Nick, that was
like flying.

One afternoon there was a ball game in the school yard. The ball went higher and higher. It landed on the roof of the gym. The ball rolled to the edge of the roof and got stuck. All the children groaned.

Timmie threw a big ball to try to move the ball that was stuck. But the ball didn't move. A teacher put Ben onto his shoulders, but Ben couldn't get the ball down.

Nick had an idea. So he left the
playground. He went into the open gym,
past the tall gym windows, and went
right to where the window pole was. He
took the pole and went back outside.

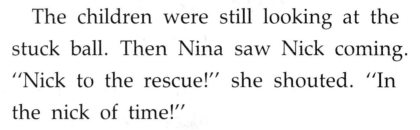

The children were still looking at the stuck ball. Then Nina saw Nick coming. "Nick to the rescue!" she shouted. "In the nick of time!"

"Excuse me, please," said Nick. He held the window pole. No one was going to take it from him! He stopped under the edge of the roof. He held the pole up and poked the ball. The ball dropped down.

"Nick to the rescue!" everyone shouted.

Nick felt as if he were flying.

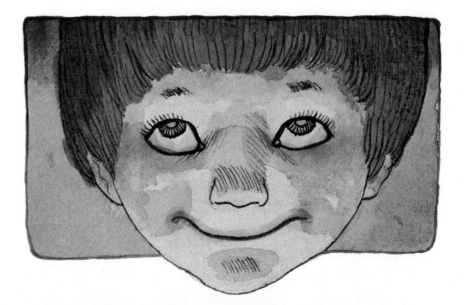

1. How did Nick feel about his new school? Why?

2. What did you think about the way the children treated Nick on his first day at school?

3. What did Nick do that the children did not do?

4. What did the children find out about helping one another?

5. What sentence tells you how Nick felt when he got the ball down?

Think and Write

Write a letter to a friend as if you are Nick. Tell your friend about your school and the people you have met.

Someone

by Carol Quinn

Someone came
To school today,
Someone new
From far away.
Someone quiet,
Someone shy,
Who watches as
We hurry by.

Someone lonely,
Someone who
Is frightened by
A place that's new.
I'll invite
That someone new
To join in
Everything I do.
And when the busy
School day ends,
Someone new
Will share my friends.

Draw Conclusions

Sometimes a story only gives clues about what is happening. When you use the clues you are given, you **draw conclusions** about what you are reading.

Read the following paragraph. Look for clues to help you draw conclusions.

The ball rolled to the edge of the roof and got stuck. Nick left the playground. He went into the open gym and went right to where the window pole was. He took the pole and went back outside.

What was Nick going to do? He was going to use the window pole to get the ball.

How did you know? He left the playground, went into the gym, and got the window pole. These are all details that give clues.

Now read this paragraph. Look for the clues that tell you where Peter is.

Peter walked and walked. He stopped and looked at the animals. Peter saw some seals. He saw some elephants, too. Peter liked the elephants best of all.

Where was Peter? How did you know this? The clues in the paragraph are *walked and walked, saw some seals*, and *saw some elephants*. These clues should have helped you know that Peter was at the zoo. Looking for clues in a story or a paragraph can help you understand what you read.

Now you are going to read a selection about a missing dog. Look for clues to help find the missing dog.

Jane Martin likes to help people solve problems. What clues does Jane use as she tries to solve the case of the missing dog?

Jane Martin, Dog Detective

by Eve Bunting

Jane pinned the sign on the pole. It said:

> Have you lost a dog?
> Let me find it for you.
> Jane Martin, Dog Detective
> 23 Oak Street
> (My treehouse is at the back.)
>
> Fee 25 cents a day

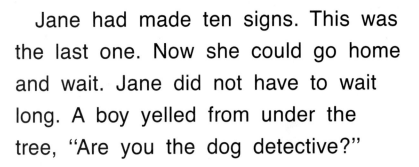

Jane had made ten signs. This was the last one. Now she could go home and wait. Jane did not have to wait long. A boy yelled from under the tree, "Are you the dog detective?"

"Yes," said Jane as she came down from her tree house. She had on her dog detective badge.

"I am Tim Wilson," the boy said. "My dog, Charlie, is missing."

Jane wrote in her notebook: Case one—find Charlie, the missing dog. "I will need to know everything about Charlie," Jane said.

"Charlie was not in his doghouse this morning," Tim told her. "Someone left this note."

Jane read the note:

> *I took Charlie. I will take good care of him.*

"We will go to your house. I will look for clues," said Jane.

Tim showed her Charlie's doghouse.

"The person who took Charlie also took his dish, his bone, and his hoop," said Tim.

Jane said, "There might be a clue here. What does Charlie do with his hoop?"

"He can push his hoop with his nose. Charlie is smart. He can even count. When I ask how old he is, he barks four times. Charlie always wins the Smartest Dog prize at the dog show. The show is next week. I hope you can find him by then."

Tim showed Jane a picture of Charlie. He was small and white.

"I am thinking," Jane said. "Someone wants to put Charlie in the show, and Charlie will get the first prize. We must see the list of the dogs that will be in the dog show."

The dog-show man told them the
names and kinds of dogs in the show.

"I need to see Rover, Biff, and
Flash," Jane said.

"You don't have to see Flash," Tim
said. "Flash is Susie's dog. He is not
a very smart dog. He barks when there
is no one at the door. When someone
is there, Flash never barks. Why did
Susie put him in the dog show?"

Jane said, "I will find Charlie. You
go home now, Tim."

She went to Rover's house. Rover had long, long ears. "You can't be Charlie," Jane said.

She went to Biff's house. Biff was very, very small. "You can't be Charlie," Jane said.

"Flash is the only dog left on the list," she thought, "and Tim knows Flash. So Susie could not change Charlie for Flash. But why would Susie put Flash . . ." Jane stopped. "Oh!" she cried. She felt like a real detective.

Jane ran to Flash's house. She rang the bell. A dog barked. Susie came to the door.

"Hi," Jane said. She showed Susie her dog detective badge. "I want to see Flash."

"Why?" Susie asked.

"I am on a big case," Jane said.

"Flash! Flash!" Susie called. No dog came. "I will have to get him," Susie said. She came back with a little dog. He could have been Charlie, but he wasn't white.

Susie put the dog down. "Sit," she said. The dog didn't sit. "Up," Susie said. The dog sat down.

"I can see that this is not Charlie," Jane said. "This dog is not very smart. He must be Flash."

Jane knew that Susie had Charlie. She thought about what Tim had told her.

"How old are you, Charlie?" she cried. From the back of the house came four barks. Charlie had answered.

"The game is over," Jane told Susie. "Bring Charlie to me."

Susie was afraid. "How did you know?" she asked Jane.

"When I rang the doorbell, a dog barked. Flash does not bark when someone comes to the door."

Just then a small white dog ran into the room. "Bark once if you are Charlie," Jane said. The little dog barked once.

"How did you get out?" Susie asked.

"He's a smart dog," Jane said.

Someone rang the doorbell. It was Tim. He ran in when Susie opened the door. Charlie ran right to Tim.

"Oh, Charlie! Charlie!" Tim said.
"I could not stay home," he told Jane.
"I followed you. Then I heard Charlie
bark. Why did you take him, Susie?"

"I was going to give Charlie back,
but first I wanted him to teach Flash
some tricks. I want Flash to be a smart
dog, too."

"That is why she took the hoop,"
Jane told Tim. "Charlie could use the
hoop to teach Flash."

"If you had asked me, I would have helped you," Tim said to Susie. "All dogs can learn. I can teach Flash. Do you want me to?"

"Yes, please," Susie said.

"Then I won't say anything to anyone," Tim said. "But you can pay Jane for finding Charlie."

Jane opened her notebook. She wrote:

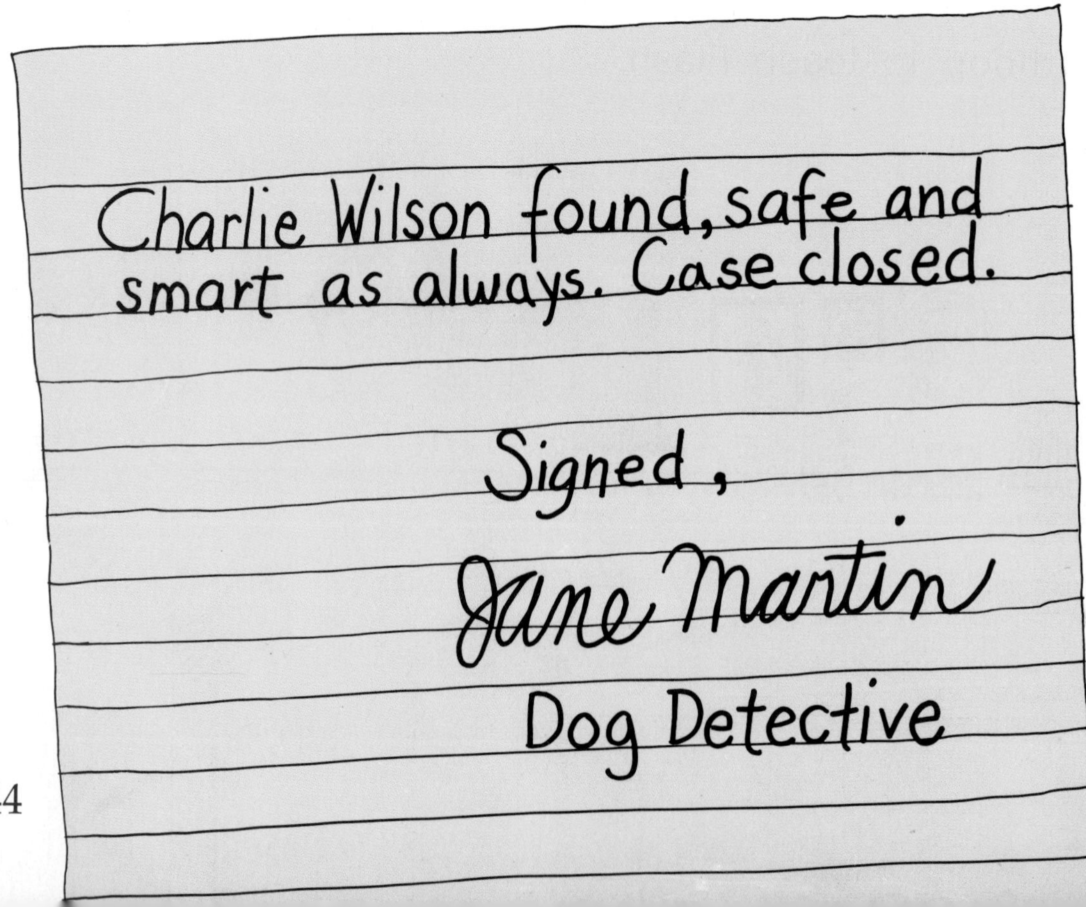

Charlie Wilson found, safe and smart as always. Case closed.

Signed,

Jane Martin

Dog Detective

1. What clues did Jane use in the case of the missing dog?

2. What was the final clue that helped Jane solve the case?

3. Do you think Susie chose the right way to teach Flash tricks? What else could she have done?

4. Where in the story did you think that Charlie was at Susie's house?

5. Jane Martin was a "good thinker." How did this help her solve the case?

Think and Write

Think about any animal other than a dog. Write three sentences that tell about the animal so someone could find it if it were lost.

Reality and Fantasy

Stories that people make up are called
fiction. If a story could be real or true,
it is called **realistic.** Made-up stories
that we think could have happened are
called **realistic fiction.** The story "Nick
Joins In" is made up, but Nick seems
like a real boy. The things he says and
does are just like the things you might
say and do.

Some stories we read could not really
happen. We call these stories **fantasy.**
Fantasy stories may be about people
who do things that could not really
happen. They may also be about animals
that can do things that only people can
do. In fantasy stories, animals may talk,
drive cars, cook, and dance.

Read the following sentences. Which would be in a realistic story? Which would be in a fantasy? Why?

1. Three bears went to a party.
2. Ben rode a yellow bike to school.

Sentence 1 is fantasy because bears can't go to a party. Sentence 2 is realistic because someone really could ride a yellow bike to school.

Now read these sentences. Decide which would be in a realistic story. Decide which would be in a fantasy. Tell why.

3. Mr. Fig used his magic hat to fly up into the sky.
4. Jane went right home after school.

As you read the next selection, try to decide if it is a realistic story or a fantasy and why.

Barkley thought he was too old to stay with the circus. Where does Barkley go? What happens to him?

Barkley

story and pictures by Syd Hoff

Barkley had a job in the circus. He did tricks with four other dogs. Barkley walked on his front legs. He walked on his back legs. The other dogs stood on Barkley's back and jumped off. If one of the dogs did something wrong, Barkley barked!

Barkley always led the way when the
dogs walked on a rope. Everyone
clapped and yelled, and Barkley took a
bow. Then he played with the children.
Barkley liked that best of all.

One day, when the four dogs jumped
on Barkley's back, it hurt! Another day,
Barkley walked too slowly. The other
dogs went in front of him. "I will be
all right," thought Barkley, but he could
not take a bow.

"I think you are getting old," said
Barkley's owner. "That happens to all of
us." The next day, Barkley's owner said,
"I don't want you to get hurt. Another
dog is taking your place."

Barkley saw the other dog doing his tricks. The other dog did them very well.

Barkley missed the clapping, and he missed the yelling. He missed the children most of all. "There must be something I can do," he thought.

Barkley tried to work with the seals, but the ball would not stay on his nose. He tried to do tricks with the elephants, but he just got in their way.

"There is nothing I can do here," he thought. So when no one was looking, Barkley left the circus.

Barkley walked and walked for a long time. He wanted some food. "If I do a trick," he thought, "maybe someone will give me a bone."

He walked on his front legs. He walked on his back legs. No one gave him a bone. He saw a bone in a trash can, but someone came and took the bone away.

Barkley saw some children playing.
He was so happy that he did some tricks
for them. The children played with him,
and they gave him food and water.

The children liked Barkley so much
that they wanted to keep him. "We
cannot keep you," said a girl. "There is
only one place for a smart dog like you."
She took Barkley back to the circus!

"Where were you?" asked his owner.
"I missed you. I didn't want you to
leave the circus. We need you to teach
young dogs your tricks."

Barkley was very happy! He started his
new job the next day. Barkley showed
his tricks to the young dogs. When a
young dog did something wrong, Barkley
barked.

Now Barkley had more time to play
with the children. He never wanted to
leave the circus again.

1. What did Barkley do after he left the circus?

2. Do you think the girl should have taken Barkley back to the circus? Why?

3. What words in the story show that the circus owner likes Barkley?

4. How did the owner solve Barkley's problem?

5. Why was teaching the young dogs tricks a good thing for Barkley to do?

Think and Write

Barkley needs a job. Write an ad that tells about all the things that he can do.

Southern California Council on
Literature for Children and
Young People

My Dog

by Myra Cohn Livingston

He didn't bark *at* anything —
    a cat,
    a bird,
    a piece of string,
    a siren or a silly toad,
    a pick-up truck along the road,
    a fence,
    a bone,
    a chewed-up shoe —
He barked because he *wanted* to.

Did you know that dogs can help people? Find out how dogs do this.

Dogs at Work

by Phyllis Hoffman

Did you know that some dogs have jobs? They do not work at a circus or do tricks at home. Their jobs are to help people.

Some dogs help blind people. Other dogs help deaf people.

The dogs that help the blind are called Seeing Eye dogs. These dogs must go to special schools where they learn many things. The person who wants the Seeing Eye dog must also go to the same school.

The school only picks special kinds of dogs. The dogs must be smart and about one year old. They must like people and listen well. They must sit, come, and stay when told.

Each Seeing Eye dog is fitted with a special bar. The dog learns to walk in front of the teacher and to cross streets. The dog must also learn not to play with other dogs when it is working.

When the blind person comes to the school, he or she must learn how to take care of the dog. The blind person must also learn to tell the dog what to do. The person and the dog work hard together. When they have learned to work with each other, the dog and its owner are ready to go home.

Dogs are also trained to help deaf people. These dogs are called hearing ear dogs. They must listen very well and must be very smart.

At school, these dogs learn to follow hand signals because many deaf people can't speak. These hand signals are the "words" that the deaf people will use to tell a dog what to do. The dogs must learn to listen for special sounds. When the doorbell rings, the dog must learn to pull the deaf person to the door. In the morning when the clock goes off, the hearing ear dog knows to wake up its owner.

Many hearing ear dogs must also learn how to tell parents if a baby is crying. A hearing ear dog learns to listen for many sounds.

Seeing Eye and hearing ear dogs are very special. They work hard to help people. They are also loving pets!

1. What are two ways that dogs help people?

2. What are two things a Seeing Eye dog must do? What are two things a hearing ear dog must do?

3. What do you think about Seeing Eye and hearing ear dogs?

4. What words did the author use to tell you that a person must learn to use a Seeing Eye dog?

Think and Write

You have read about dogs at work. What other animals have jobs? Choose one animal and write three sentences about it. Where does the animal work? What job does the animal do?

Thinking About "Stepping Stones"

In "Stepping Stones," you read about people and animals who tried doing new things. It took Ronald some time to get used to having glasses. Nick was afraid before he went to school, but liked it in a short time. Barkley was sad about getting older, but he found a new job that made him happy.

Taking a step in a new direction may be a problem, but it may turn out to be lots of fun. It helps to take things one step at a time. As you read other stories, think about the people in the stories and what they learn by taking a step in a new direction.

1. What new thing did Ronald Morgan need that Benjamin Franklin needed, too?

2. How are Nick and Ronald Morgan alike? How are they different?

3. Would Barkley have been a good dog to train for one of the jobs in "Dogs at Work"? Why?

4. Why might the circus owner have called Jane Martin about Barkley?

Unit 2

Earth and Sky

In "Earth and Sky," you will learn many things about our world.

You will learn about how the sun gives us food and light here on the earth. You will also read about the special trip a raindrop takes. You will read an old tale that tells about how the sun keeps the earth warm.

As you read "Earth and Sky," think about ways that the earth and the sky work together. See what different people think about the earth and sky.

Read on Your Own

The Way to Start a Day *by Byrd Baylor. Scribner's.* This book tells how people around the world greet the day.

Harold and the Purple Crayon *by Crockett Johnson. Harper.* Harold draws himself a journey and gets lost on the way. When he sees the moon, he remembers that it always shines through his window, so he can follow its light home.

The Blue Rocket Fun Show, or Friends Forever! *by Thomas P. Lewis. Macmillan.* Leslie finds out that her friend Nikki is an alien from outer space, but Leslie remains a loyal friend and learns many new things.

Rainy Sunday *by Eleanor Schick. Dial.* Jill spends a pleasant rainy day with her parents both indoors and outside.

Why Do Grown-ups Have All the Fun?
by Marisabina Russe. Greenwillow. Hannah
cannot sleep because she imagines the
grown-ups are having so much fun doing
things she likes to do.

Rain Drop Splash *by Alvin Tresselt. Lothrop.*
The raindrops grow until they become a
puddle, then a pond, a lake, and a river
and do not stop until they reach the sea.

What the Moon Saw *by Brian Wildsmith.*
Oxford. The sun brags to the moon of the
many things she sees, but only the moon
can see the dark.

Say It! *by Charlotte Zolotow. Greenwillow.* A
little girl and her mother show their love
for each other in many ways during a
walk on a windy autumn day.

Clyde doesn't like the nighttime because he is afraid of the dark. Why is Clyde afraid? How do his parents help him solve his problem?

Clyde Monster

by Robert L. Crowe

Clyde wasn't a very, very old monster, but he was growing uglier every day. He lived in a large forest with his parents.

Father Monster was a big, big monster
and very ugly, which was good. Friends
and family sometimes make fun of a pretty
monster. Mother Monster was even
uglier. All in all, they were a picture
family—as monsters go.

Clyde lived in a cave. That is, at
night he was supposed to live in a cave.
In the daytime, he played in the forest.
He did monster things like breathing fire
at the lake.

He also did Clyde things like jumping
up and down. This made large holes in
the ground. He was always bumping into
things, too.

When Clyde was supposed to go to his
cave and sleep, the problem started. He
didn't want to go to his cave.

"Why?" asked his mother. "Why won't you go to your cave?"

"Because," answered Clyde, "I'm afraid of the dark."

"Afraid?" asked his father. "A monster of mine afraid? What are you afraid of?"

"People," said Clyde. "I'm afraid there are people in there who will get me."

"That's silly," said his father.
"Come, I'll show you." His father breathed out so much fire that it lit up the cave. "There. Did you see any people?"

"No, but they may be hiding under a rock. They'll jump out and get me after I'm sleeping," answered Clyde.

"That is silly," said his mother. "There are no people here. Even if there were, they wouldn't hurt you."

"They wouldn't?" asked Clyde.

"No," said his mother. "Would you ever hide in the dark under a bed to scare a boy or girl?"

"No!" answered Clyde, upset that his mother would even think that.

"Well, people wouldn't hide and scare
you. A long time ago monsters and people
made a deal," said his father. "Monsters
won't scare people—and people won't
scare monsters."

"Really?" Clyde asked.

"Yes," said his mother. "Do you know of a monster who was ever scared by a person?"

"No," answered Clyde after some thought.

"Do you know of any boys or girls who were ever scared by a monster?"

"No," he answered.

"There!" said his mother. "Now off to bed."

"No more talk about being scared by people," said his father.

"All right, but could you keep the rock open just a little?" Clyde asked as he went into his cave.

1. Why was Clyde afraid of the dark?

2. How did his parents help him not to be afraid?

3. What did you think about a monster being afraid of people?

4. Where in the story did you think that Clyde was still afraid?

5. Why do you think people are sometimes afraid of the dark?

**Think
and
Write**

Think about how Clyde felt about the dark. How could you help him with his problem? What could you do to make him feel better? Write a story that tells how you could help Clyde Monster not to be afraid of the dark.

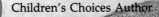

Night is Here

by Jack Prelutsky

Night is here, and night is there,
and night is all around,
I feel its presence everywhere,
and yet it makes no sound.

And so it's time to close my eyes,
and dream the night away,
until the sun lights up the skies,
and welcomes back the day.

Cause and Effect

Read the following paragraph from "Clyde Monster."

He also did Clyde things like jumping up and down. This made large holes in the ground.

What did Clyde do? He did Clyde things like jumping up and down. What happened when he did this? This made large holes in the ground. Clyde's jumping up and down is the *reason* there were holes in the ground. The *reason* something happens is the **cause.** The holes in the ground are *what happened,* or the **effect.**

Read the following sentence.

Nick was sad because Robin moved away.

The sentence tells that Nick was sad. This is what happened, or the effect. The sentence also tells the reason why, or the cause, for Nick's being sad: Robin moved away.

Now read the following sentences. Find the cause and the effect in each sentence by asking what is happening or the effect, and the reason why it is happening or the cause.

1. Sue turned on the light because the room was dark.
2. The room was sunny, so Sue pulled down the shade.

Looking for causes and effects in stories can help you better understand what you read. As you read the next selection, try to find some causes and effects.

The sun is far away from our planet, Earth. How does the sun help our planet?

Sun Up, Sun Down

by Gail Gibbons

The sun wakes me up. It comes up in the east and shines in my window. It lights up my room. It makes my room warm. It colors the clouds and the sky. I get up and get dressed.

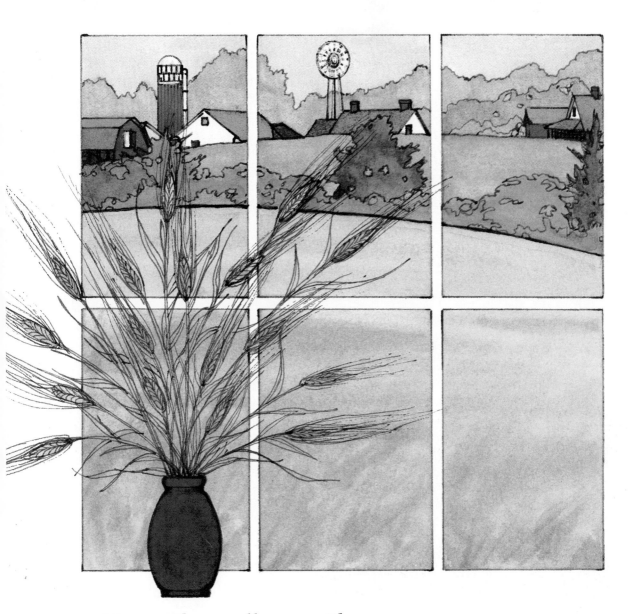

My mother calls me. She wants me
to eat my cereal. It is made from
whole wheat. My dad tells me the sun
helps the wheat grow. He says the sun
helps plants and trees grow big and tall.

While I'm eating my cereal, I ask my
parents a question: "How far away is
the sun?" My mother tells me it is very
far away from our planet, Earth. She
says that the sun is a star. It looks
bigger than the other stars because
it is nearer to Earth than other stars.

My dad says the sun keeps our planet warm. He says Earth would be dark and cold if there were no sun. Nothing could live on Earth without the sun.

My mom tells me why some days are short and others are long. She says that in the summer it is warm. The sun is high in the sky, and the days are long. In winter, it is cold. The sun is low in the sky and the days are shorter.

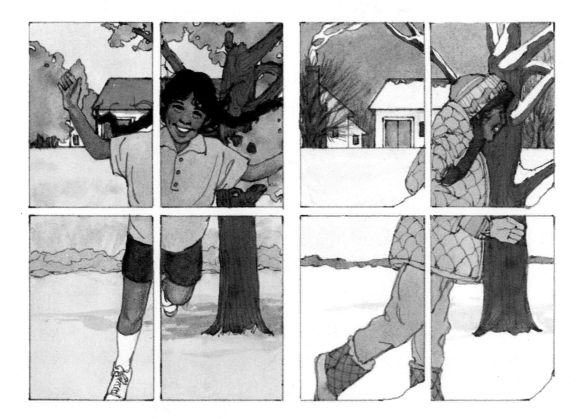

My dad also tells me that the sun will shine on the other side of our planet while I'm sleeping. He says that Earth spins as it moves around the sun. It makes one full spin every day.

When the side of the planet Earth we live on faces the sun, it is day. When our side is turned away from the sun, it is night. At night, the sky is dark. It is time to sleep.

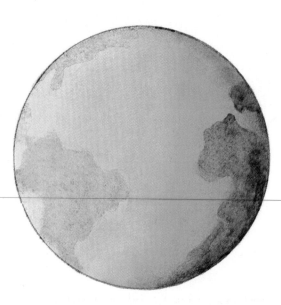

Discuss the Selection

1. How does the sun help people and plants on Earth?

2. How important is the sun to people on Earth?

3. When did you first learn that the sun is a very big star?

4. What did you think when you read that the earth turns?

Think and Write

Think about what it would be like if the sun stopped shining. Write about some of the things that you think would happen to plants and people if there were no sun.

What does Caroline Porcupine have to do to get a new job on the Claws and Paws *newspaper? Do you think she will get the job? Why?*

Forecast

by Malcolm Hall

Stan Groundhog stood up. The whole party was for him. After many years, Stan was going away. He was leaving his job as weather forecaster for the *Claws and Paws* newspaper.

Theodore Cat, who was the owner of the paper, said, "Stan, give us your last weather forecast."

"All right," said Stan. He went to the window and looked outside. Next he looked down at his shadow. Then he said, "It will be warm and sunny all afternoon. It won't rain. Now I have to be going. Thanks for the party."

With that, there was a crack of lightning. All the lights in the office went out. Next came the thunder. Ka—ka—kabloom!!! Then the rain started to come down.

Stan waved good-bye and left.

Theodore looked around the room. "Does anyone know a groundhog who needs a job?"

Caroline Porcupine asked, "Does the forecaster have to be a groundhog?"

"Yes," said Theodore. "Everyone knows that groundhogs know when spring is coming by looking at their shadows. That's why I want another groundhog as a weather forecaster."

Caroline said, "I want the job. You see, I know a lot about the weather. Last year, I took a class in weather forecasting."

"Is that so?" said Theodore.

"Yes it is," said Caroline right back. "I can make real forecasts. If you let me, I will show you."

"All right," said Theodore. "Let's make a bet. You forecast the weather for all of next week. If you are right five days in a row, I will give you the job. If not, I'll get a groundhog."

"Theodore, I'll take your bet," said Caroline.

The next day, Caroline took her weather instruments to work. She had instruments for all kinds of things.

All that morning, Caroline set up her instruments. One by one, the animals stopped working. They walked over to Caroline's desk and watched her. By afternoon she was ready. She wrote down everything that her instruments told her.

Then Caroline looked up. "I am ready to make my forecast for the week. Today is Monday. It will be nice for the rest of the day. Tuesday, it will be sunny and warm. Wednesday, it will be cold. Thursday, it will rain." The animals looked at each other and smiled. So far, the forecast seemed good—maybe Caroline would be right!

Caroline went on, "On Friday, it will be cold in the morning, with snow in the afternoon." The animals were surprised.

Theodore laughed. "Snow? Did you say snow? Caroline, look outside. The sky is bright blue, and it's been very hot for weeks and weeks."

Caroline answered, "My instruments say it will snow on Friday."

"All right," said Theodore. "If it snows on Friday, you will get the job. I'm going to keep on looking for a groundhog, however."

On Thursday it rained the whole day. Theodore came in very wet. He thought, "Caroline's been right four days in a row. Maybe I should give her the job even if it doesn't snow on Friday."

Friday started out cold, just as Caroline had said it would. By noon, however, there was still no snow.

Theodore sat in his office, looking out the window. If he had turned his head, he would have seen Frank Beaver and Oscar Raccoon run past his door. Each one had a large sack. They were headed for the roof.

A little later, Theodore looked
outside. A white flake had just floated
down past his window! Then came
another flake . . . and another . . . and
another! He jumped up. "Snow! It's
really snowing!" he shouted.

Theodore ran out of his office.
"Caroline! It's snowing! You are the
greatest forecaster ever! I take back
everything I said."

Theodore was so happy that he just
about hugged Caroline. You never hug a
porcupine, however. So he took Caroline
into his office. "See! Look out the
window. It is snowing!" he said.

Caroline looked outside. "That doesn't look like snow to me," she said.

"Yes, it is," said Theodore. He opened the window. Flakes started to come in. One landed on his nose. "Aaaa—choo!!!" Theodore looked very surprised.

"Let me see that snowflake." He took the flake and held it up to the light. "I thought so. This is a feather!"

Theodore looked up on the roof. He saw Frank and Oscar holding sacks that had feathers in them.

"Come down from there!" shouted
Theodore. "Come into my office."

In Theodore's office, a little later,
the animals all looked out the window.
Flakes were coming down again. This
time it was *really* snowing.

"That's *real* snow!" said Theodore.

"Yes, it is!" said Caroline. "I told
you it would snow."

1. What did Caroline have to do to get the job of weather forecaster?

2. How did Caroline predict the weather?

3. What part of the story did you think was the funniest? Why?

4. Where in the story did you know what the animals thought about Caroline's Friday forecast?

5. Why did Theodore have doubts about Caroline's forecast?

Think and Write

Think about when Theodore almost hugged Caroline. Write a paragraph that tells what would have happened if Theodore really had hugged her.

Change in the Weather

by Ilo Orleans

I think it would be very good
To have some snow and sleet
In summer when
We need it most
To drive away the heat.

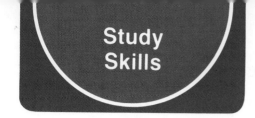

Maps

Maps are used to show many things. Street maps show you how to find your way around your town. Weather maps show you what the weather forecast is for many places.

If you know what the weather forecast is, you can plan your day. You will know to take an umbrella if the weather map shows that it is going to rain where you live. Because the weather changes every day, weather maps also change every day.

Look at the weather map on the next page. It shows what the weather forecast is for one day in the United States.

Below the map is the **legend,** or key, for the map. The legend helps you read the map. Each picture in the legend stands for something. The word next to each picture tells what that picture means.

By looking at the legend and the weather map, you can see what the weather forecast is for one day in the United States.

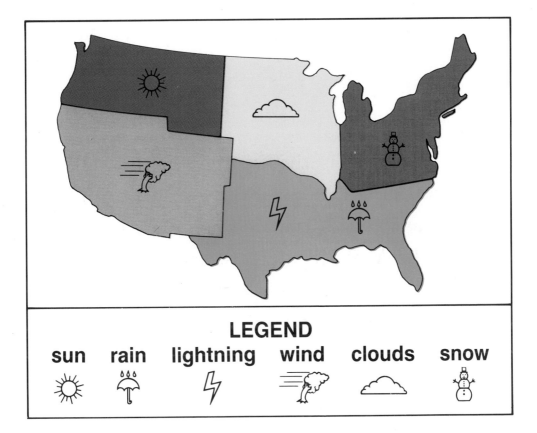

LEGEND

sun   rain   lightning   wind   clouds   snow

Use the legend to help you read the map on the next page. What is the weather in the blue zone? It is sunny. How do you know this? There is a sun in the blue zone on the map. What is the weather in the red zone? It is snowing. How do you know this? There is a snowman in the red zone on the map.

Read the following questions about the weather map. Use the map and the legend to help you answer the questions.

1. What is the weather in the yellow zone?
2. What is the weather in the green zone?
3. What is the weather in the orange zone?

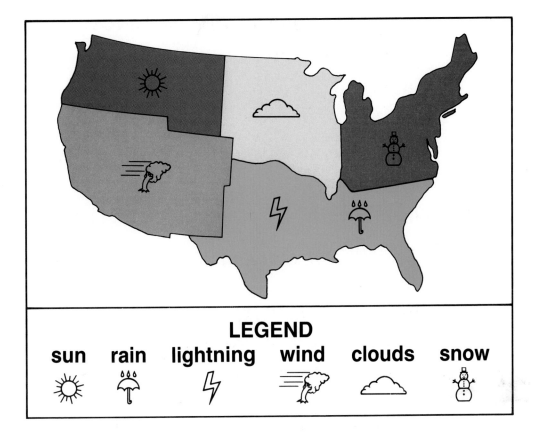

LEGEND

| sun | rain | lightning | wind | clouds | snow |

Remember, the legend of a map helps you read the map. Each picture stands for something that is on the map. By looking at the map and the map legend, you will know the weather forecast.

Raindrops fall from clouds in the sky. What happens to a raindrop after it falls to the ground?

Splash

by Ronda Maseman

This is the story of a raindrop. The raindrop's name is Splash.

Splash slides down the trunk of a tree. It lands on a little plant at the bottom of the tree. Splash slips down a leaf. It goes into a little pool made by many other raindrops.

Splash sinks into the ground, under
little roots, and slides around some rocks.
Splash stops. It rests on one of the big
tree roots. Then it is pulled inside the
root. Pop! Slowly Splash goes up the
root. Then Splash moves up through
all parts of the tree. Splash helps to
feed the tree.

At the top of the tree, Splash turns
into a gas and goes back to the clouds.
In the clouds, Splash becomes a
raindrop. Splash rests in a cloud for
a while.

Other raindrops come up to the cloud, too. Soon there are lots of raindrops in the cloud.

This time the cloud goes over a mountain. It is very cold on top of the mountain. The water in the cloud freezes and turns into ice and snow. Now Splash becomes a very pretty snowflake. Splash and the other snowflakes fall on top of the mountain.

The hot sun melts the snow. The melted snow and Splash then slide down the mountain. Splash and the melted snow turn into a little brook. The brook gets larger and larger and moves into a river.

By now some of the other raindrops in the river have turned back into a gas. They go up to the clouds while Splash is still having fun floating around in the big river.

Splash moves on down the river to the waterworks to be cleaned. After the water is cleaned, Splash and the water are sent through pipes to people's homes to be used.

Splash goes into a house and is pushed out through a long hose. This hose is being used to water the flowers. Now Splash falls onto one of the flowers. The sun gets hotter and hotter, and Splash turns into a gas. Soon Splash goes up into a cloud to come down as rain another day.

1. What happens to Splash after it falls from the first cloud?

2. How does Splash help the tree?

3. Did any part of Splash's trip surprise you? Why?

4. When did you first think that Splash would keep turning into gas, then water, and then fall to Earth over and over?

5. Splash changed many times. Name three ways Splash changed.

Think and Write

Think about the places that Splash went. Decide which place Splash liked best. Write a paragraph that tells which place Splash liked the best and why.

Owl does not want the moon to follow him home from the seashore. Does Owl change his mind?

Owl and the Moon

story and pictures by Arnold Lobel

One night, Owl went down to the seashore. He sat on a large rock and looked out at the waves. Everything was dark. Then a small tip of the moon came up over the edge of the sea.

Owl watched the moon. It climbed higher and higher into the sky. Soon the whole, round moon was shining.

Owl sat on the rock and looked up at the moon for a long time.

"If I am looking at you, moon, then you must be looking back at me. We must be very good friends."

The moon did not answer, but Owl said, "I will come back and see you again, moon. But now I must go home."

Owl walked down the path. He looked up at the sky. The moon was still there. It was following him.

"No, no, moon," said Owl. "It is kind of you to light my way. But you must stay up over the sea where you look so fine."

Owl walked on a little farther. He looked at the sky again. There was the moon coming right along with him.

"Dear moon," said Owl, "you really must not come home with me. My house is small. You would not fit through the door. And I have nothing to give you for supper."

Owl kept on walking. The moon sailed after him over the tops of the trees.

"Moon," said Owl, "I think that you do not hear me."

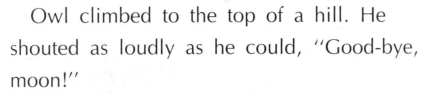

Owl climbed to the top of a hill. He shouted as loudly as he could, "Good-bye, moon!"

The moon went behind some clouds. Owl looked and looked. The moon was gone.

"It is always a little sad to say good-bye to a friend," said Owl.

Owl came home. He put on his pajamas and went to bed. The room was very dark. Owl was still feeling sad.

All at once, Owl's bedroom was filled
with silver light.

Owl looked out of the window. The
moon was coming from behind the clouds.

"Moon, you have followed me all the
way home. What a good, round friend you
are!" said Owl. Then Owl put his head on
the pillow and closed his eyes.

The moon was shining down through the
window. Owl did not feel sad at all.

1. Why didn't Owl want the moon to follow him home?

2. Did Owl change his mind? Why?

3. What did you think when the moon went behind the cloud?

4. When did you find out that the moon really had followed Owl home?

5. Owl thought of the moon as his friend. How did the moon help him feel better?

**Think
and
Write**

Think about what the moon might have said to Owl if it could talk. Write a story that tells what the two friends might have said to each other.

Long ago, people made up this story to tell why there is day and night. What promise did the sun make? Why?

How the Sun Made a Promise and Kept It

A Canadian Indian myth retold by Margery Bernstein and Janet Kobrin

Long, long ago, there were rivers and lakes. There was dry land.

Sometimes Earth was a beautiful place for people to live. Other times, however, it was not a good place to live. In those days, the sun went wherever it wanted to go. It didn't always come near Earth. When the sun was away, Earth was dark and cold.

One of the people who lived then and who thought about Earth was named Weese-ke-jak. "I must do something," he said. "We need the sun for light and to warm us."

Weese-ke-jak thought and thought. At last he had an idea.

"The next time the sun comes near Earth," Weese-ke-jak thought, "I will catch it in a net. I will keep it close to Earth. Then Earth will always be warm and light."

Weese-ke-jak made a net out of ropes. The net was very large. Then Weese-ke-jak waited.

When the sun came near Earth
again, Weese-ke-jak took his net. He
swung it around and around. Then he
threw it up into the sky. The net
dropped over the sun. The sun was
trapped!

Weese-ke-jak pulled the net with the
sun in it down to Earth. He tied the
ropes to a tree stump.

The sun pulled and pulled. It could
not get itself free. "Weese-ke-jak, let me
go," begged the sun. "Let me go! Why
do you keep me in this net?"

"I have trapped you so that I can
keep you near Earth," answered
Weese-ke-jak. "Now Earth will be
warm and light all the time."

Weese-ke-jak would not let the sun
go. He had pulled the sun too near
Earth, however. It began to get hotter
and hotter.

Soon it was so hot that the birds
flew down out of the sky to see what
had happened. The animals came out of
the forests.

"If it gets any hotter," thought Weese-ke-jak, "everything will burn. I must let the sun out of the net. Maybe I can make the sun promise not to go too far away."

Then Weese-ke-jak called to the sun. "I might let you go, but you must promise something first."

"I will promise anything you say, Weese-ke-jak," answered the sun. "Just let me go."

"Well . . ." said Weese-ke-jak, "will you keep your promise?"

"I will keep my promise," cried the sun. "What must I do?"

"You must never go too far away," said Weese-ke-jak. "You may come close to the edges of Earth, but only in the morning and at night. In the daytime, you must come just near enough to warm Earth."

"I will do as you say," said the sun. "Now, please let me go!"

Weese-ke-jak went over to free the sun. The sun was so hot that he could not get near the net.

So Weese-ke-jak called to the animals. "I cannot get close to the sun," he said. "Can anyone help me?"

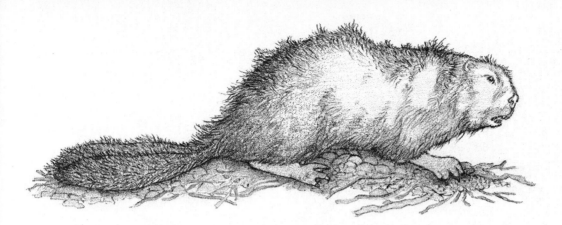

A few of the animals were brave.
They tried to help Weese-ke-jak.

First, Deer tried to free the sun.
Then Fox tried. Then Otter tried. They
could not get near enough. The sun was
too hot.

Then Beaver said, "I will try." In
those days, Beaver did not look the
same as he looks now. He had only a
few small teeth. His fur was rough. He
was not very beautiful, but he was very
brave.

Beaver ran to the net. He began to
bite the tough ropes that held the net.
The sun was very, very hot, but Beaver
did not give up.

At last, Beaver bit through the tough rope. The sun was free! It rose up from Earth like a balloon.

Earth became cooler. Weese-ke-jak and the animals were happy. They ran to thank Beaver.

Beaver, however, was not happy. The heat from the sun had burned his coat. He had very little fur left.

Weese-ke-jak said, "Don't be sad, Beaver. Because you were so brave, I will give you two presents."

Weese-ke-jak gave Beaver a beautiful
new fur coat. He gave Beaver a new set
of fine, sharp teeth.

Weese-ke-jak did not put any fur on
Beaver's tail. "Beaver's tail will never
have any fur," said Weese-ke-jak, "so
everyone will remember how brave he
was. They will remember that he set
the sun free."

The sun remembered, too. And in all
the days of the world since then, the
sun has kept this promise.

1. What promise did the sun make? Why?

2. Why did Weese-ke-jak throw a net around the sun?

3. What did Beaver do to help?

4. What did you think of Beaver as he was biting through the rope?

5. What part tells how Beaver looked before he helped to free the sun?

6. How did you know that catching the sun was not a good idea?

Think and Write

Myths are written to tell about things that people don't understand. Write your own myth to tell why you think the sun shines.

Thinking About "Earth and Sky"

In "Earth and Sky," you learned many things about your world. You learned that the sun's light warms the earth and makes things grow. You also learned about what happens to a raindrop after it falls from the sky. You read that Clyde was afraid of the dark and how Owl made friends with the moon.

The earth and sky help each other in many ways. What other new and surprising things did you learn about the earth and sky? As you read other stories, try to find out more about how the earth and sky work together.

1. Why would Clyde Monster have been happy if the moon had followed him home?

2. How are the moon in "Owl and the Moon" and the sun in "How the Sun Made a Promise and Kept It" different?

3. How might the sun and a raindrop like Splash help wheat grow?

4. How are Frank Beaver in "Forecast" and Beaver in "How the Sun Made a Promise and Kept It" alike?

Unit 3

Kaleidoscopes

Have you ever seen a kaleidoscope? Kaleidoscopes have tiny bits of colored glass at the end of a long tube. As you turn the tube, the colors change and make pictures. The pictures in a kaleidoscope are always changing.

In "Kaleidoscopes," you will read about many things and people who change. Some of the changes are easy to see. People may change in the way they think about things. They may find out that things are not what they seem to be. As you read "Kaleidoscopes," think about the changes that take place in each story.

Read on Your Own

The Toad Hunt *by Janet Chenery. Harper.* Two boys learn a lot about frogs, toads, and birds on a nature hike and picnic.

George Told Kate *by Kay Chorao. Dutton.* A little elephant is worried by her older brother's teasing until she catches on.

Jim Meets the Thing *by Miriam Cohen. Greenwillow.* Jim thinks he is the only one who is afraid of anything until an ugly bug scares one of his classmates.

Hattie Be Quiet, Hattie Be Good *by Dick Gackenbach. Harper.* Hattie Rabbit tries to help her mother, but when she tries to sit quietly, her mother thinks she is sick.

Anansi the Spider *by Gerald McDermott. Holt.* This folktale is about Anansi, a cunning hero in African culture, and his six sons.

Alligators Are Awful *by David McPhail. Doubleday.* Surely, we do not know anyone with such terrible manners as these alligators!

Three Up a Tree *by James Marshall. Dial.* Lolly, Spider, and Sam entertain each other with stories. They like the stories so much, they tell them again.

Pierre, a Cautionary Tale *by Maurice Sendak. Harper.* Pierre, a very naughty boy, learns to care after he is eaten by a lion and saved by his parents. He then becomes the lion's friend.

How do three days in the library change Beatrice? What doesn't change?

Beatrice Doesn't Want To

by Laura Joffe Numeroff

Beatrice didn't like books. She didn't even like to read. More than that, she hated going to the library. But that's where her brother Henry had to take her three afternoons in a row.

Henry had to do a report on dinosaurs. Henry also had to look after Beatrice.

"Why don't you get some books?"
Henry said when they got to the library.

"I don't want to," Beatrice said.

"Look at how many books there are!"
Henry tried.

"I don't want to," Beatrice said again.

"Then what do you want to do?"
Henry asked her.

"I want to watch you," she said.

"I have to work," said Henry.

"I'll watch until you're finished," she
said.

"I give up," Henry said.

Henry worked on his report. Beatrice sat in a chair and watched him. Henry tried not to notice her.

The second day, Beatrice didn't even want to go inside. "Come on, Bea," Henry said.

"I don't want to," Beatrice told him.

"I have to work," said Henry.

"I just want to sit outside," Beatrice answered.

"All right," said Henry, "but don't move until I come out." Beatrice promised. Henry went inside to do his report.

Suddenly Henry felt drops of water.
He didn't know where they were coming
from. Then he felt someone tap his
shoulder. Henry turned around, and
there was Beatrice. She was soaking wet.
"It's raining," she said.

"I give up," said Henry.

It was still raining the third day.
Beatrice had to go inside this time. She
followed Henry around while he looked
for more books.

"Can I hold some?" Beatrice asked.

Henry gave her some books to hold.

"They're too heavy!" Beatrice yelled. Suddenly the heavy books dropped onto her foot, and she began to cry.

"I really do give up!" said Henry. "Look, Bea, I've got to finish this report. Please!" Henry begged her.

"Henry," said Beatrice, "could I have some water?"

They went down a hall to look for some water. Suddenly Henry saw a sign. This was it!

The librarian
will read

"Alfred Mouse Has a
Brand New House"
today
in the children's room
4:00

"Come on," said Henry.

"I don't want to," Beatrice said.

"That's too bad!" shouted Henry.

Before she knew it, Beatrice was in a room full of boys and girls. Henry walked out just as she started to say, "I don't want . . ."

"Hello. My name is Wanda. This is the second time I've heard this story," said the girl in the next chair.

"Big deal!" said Beatrice.

"Alfred Mouse lived in a brand new house," the librarian began to read. She held the book up so everyone could see the pictures. Beatrice looked out the window.

"Alfred Mouse also had new skates," the librarian went on.

Beatrice loved to skate. She looked at the librarian. "But Alfred's mother wasn't too happy when he skated through the house," the librarian read.

The boys and girls laughed.

Beatrice smiled. She thought about the time she had tried skating in her own house. Then Beatrice laughed. She listened to the whole story.

When the story was over, Beatrice went up to the librarian. "May I see that book, please?" she asked.

"Yes," said the librarian. Beatrice sat down in a chair and looked at each picture over and over. Suddenly she felt someone tapping her shoulder.

"Time to go," Henry said in her ear.

Beatrice kept looking at the pictures and didn't notice him. Henry put Beatrice's hat on her head. "We have to go home now," he said.

Beatrice kept on looking at the pictures.

"Come on, Bea," Henry said.

"I don't want to," Beatrice told him.

1. How did Beatrice change on the last day in the library?

2. How did Beatrice stay the same from beginning to end?

3. How did Henry finally get to do his report on dinosaurs?

4. What words in the story tell that Henry needed help with Beatrice?

5. What part of the story did you think was the funniest? Why?

Think and Write

Think about a book that you like. Draw a picture that shows something that happened in the book. Write three sentences that tell about the book.

Main Idea and Details

As you read a paragraph, think about what the paragraph tells you. Often, one sentence tells you what the whole paragraph is about. That sentence is the **main idea.** Other sentences in the paragraph tell you more about the main idea. Those sentences give you **details.**
Read the following paragraph from "Beatrice Doesn't Want To."

Beatrice didn't like books. She didn't even like to read. More than that, she hated going to the library. But that's where her brother Henry had to take her three afternoons in a row.

What is the main idea of the
paragraph? The main idea is that
Beatrice didn't like books.

What are the details in the paragraph?
The details are that Beatrice didn't like
books, she hated going to the library,
and her brother had to take her there
for three days in a row.

Now read the following paragraph and
look for its main idea.

Our class is going to put on a
play. Carla will be the wise owl.
Ed will be the friendly elephant.
Kim is going to be the ugly
monster. Rick will be the king
who chases the monster away.

What is the main idea? The main idea
is that our class is going to put on a
play. Find four details that tell about
the main idea.

As you read, look for main ideas and
details in paragraphs. This will help you
understand what you are reading.

People tell stories and listen to stories every day. How did people tell stories long ago? How has storytelling changed?

Tell Me a Story

by Donald Cooper

People have been telling stories for a very long time. Long before there were books, there were storytellers.

Many years ago, stories were often made up to tell why things happened. Sometimes the stories were about real things and people. Often the stories had a lesson in them.

In Africa, storytellers told stories only at night. The children sat in a circle around a fire in the moonlight. The storyteller sometimes carried a net. In it were small bones, feathers, and bits of glass. One child picked something from the net. Then the storyteller told a story about it.

Everyone could see the African storyteller as he stood inside the circle. Each time a new person or animal spoke in the story, the storyteller changed the way he spoke. Sometimes he beat out the sounds of the story on a drum.

American Indian storytellers told their stories at night, too. Sometimes the Indian storyteller gave small gifts to the children when the story was over. This was to thank the children for giving up a night to listen to the story.

Other Indian storytellers gave corn to children before story time. The Indians thought that if the children ate the corn as the story was being told, the meaning of the story would be clear.

In Mexico, most stories told about how or why things happened. Storytellers from Mexico often began a story by saying it was a tale from long ago. The storyteller ended the story by saying, "I saw this with my own eyes!"

In China, pictures were sometimes used to tell a story. There were different pictures for each part of the story. The storyteller pointed to one picture at a time while telling the story.

Today, most stories can be read in books, but storytelling is still important. Some libraries have a special storytelling time. Sometimes storytellers visit schools.

Storytelling helps people reach out to others. Storytellers help to bring wonderful stories to life. Wherever in the world there are children, someone will always say to them, "Let me tell you a story."

1. How did people tell stories long ago?

2. How has storytelling changed?

3. Why did storytellers make up stories long ago?

4. Which storyteller seemed most interesting to you? Tell why.

5. What words on page 150 let you know that storytelling is still being done?

6. How can you tell that the author of this article thinks storytelling is important?

Think and Write

Think about a special place that you have been. Write a story that tells about your trip. Tell your story to the class.

Christopher Award Author

A prince wants to change his life. He thinks he will be happier living a simpler life. What does the prince find out?

The Simple Prince

adapted from a book by Jane Yolen

There was once a prince who wanted to live a simple life. So he clapped his hands three times to call his servants.

"Bring me some simple clothes," he yelled. "I am going out into the world to live the simple life." So the servants found a plain suit and a plain hat as well.

The prince clapped his hands three
times and told his servants to bring him
a simple picnic lunch to eat on his way.
Then he rode for a long time. At last, he
came to the house of a simple farmer.

The prince got off his horse and went
to the door. He clapped his hands three
times. Nothing happened. He tapped his
foot. Then he shouted, "Open up!" The
door was opened. The farmer looked out.

"I have come to live the simple life," said the prince. He walked inside.

The farmer looked at his wife. She looked at the prince. The prince did not notice. He sat down on a chair and clapped his hands three times. "I want some cheese and a cup of tea," the prince said.

The farmer looked at his wife. She shook her head. The farmer just smiled.

The farmer cut the prince some cheese.
Then the farmer said: "Cheese and tea.
That is simple. Here is the cheese. As for
the tea, we need fire and water. First I
must saw the wood for the fire. It is
simple. Come with me."

The prince went outside with the farmer.
They found some wood. They sawed and
they sawed and they sawed some more. At
last the prince cried out, "Enough! Enough!
I can do no more."

"We are done," said the farmer. He filled the prince's arms with wood and led him back to the house. Then the farmer made the fire. The prince sat down again.

"Now it is time to get the water," said the farmer's wife. "It is simple. Come with me."

So the prince followed the farmer's wife to the well. Arm over arm, he pulled the pail up. He poured the water from the pail into a pitcher. Then he pulled up more pails of water. He poured the water into three pitchers. At last the prince cried, "Enough! Enough! I can do no more."

"We are done," said the farmer's wife.
She gave the prince a pitcher for each
hand. She put one on his head, too. Then
she led him back to the house.

The farmer's wife put the water into
a pot and put the pot on the fire. When
it was hot, she made tea. But the prince
had worked so hard, he was two times as
hungry as before. He clapped his hands
three times and said, "Bring me some
bread and butter with my tea."

"That is simple enough," said the farmer. "But butter comes from milk, and milk comes from a cow. Come with me."

So the prince followed the farmer to the cow. There the prince held the pail while the farmer milked the cow. The cow's tail hit the prince's face. The cow's feet kicked the prince's legs. At last the prince cried, "Enough! Enough! I can do no more."

"It is done," said the farmer.

Back in the house, the farmer made the prince churn, and churn, and churn the milk into butter. When the butter was finished, the prince fell back on the chair. He clapped his hands three times. "My butter needs some bread," he said.

"That is simple," said the farmer's wife. "But first we must bake it. Come with me to help."

So she gave the prince some dough. He patted the dough. He pushed the dough. He pulled the dough. He punched the dough. At last the prince cried, "Enough! Enough! I can do no more."

"It's done," said the farmer's wife.
Then she baked the dough.

The prince was so tired from all his
simple work that he went to sleep. He slept
through the bread-baking and supper. He
woke up the next morning. He felt very
tired. He tried to clap his hands—one
time, two times, three times. His hands
hurt from all the work he had done.

"Please," he asked, "may I have
something to eat?"

"It's simple," the farmer's wife said.
Before she could finish, the prince
jumped up from the chair.

"Enough! Enough!" he cried. "I can live
no more of the simple life. It is much too
hard for me!"

The prince ran out the door, climbed on
his horse, and raced back home as fast as
he could go. His servants helped him off
his horse, and the prince said, "Thank you."

Then he really wanted something to eat. So he asked, "Please, may I have some bread and butter?"

His servants were happy to be asked so nicely. They went quickly to get the bread and butter and a pitcher of milk.

From that day to this, the prince lived happily. He never again clapped his hands for anything. He was always careful to say "please" and "thank you." It was so much simpler that way.

1. Was the prince happier living a simple life? Why?

2. How did the prince learn about the simple life?

3. What did you think about the way the farmer and his wife treated the prince?

4. What happened that made the prince go back to his castle?

5. What made you think that the prince learned his lesson?

Think about how the prince felt when he went home. Pretend you are the prince. Write a thank-you note to the farmer and his wife. Tell about what you learned and how you changed.

Politeness

by A. A. Milne

Lewis Carroll Shelf Award

If people ask me,
I always tell them:
"Quite well, thank you. I'm very glad to say."
If people ask me,
I always answer,
"Quite well, thank you, how are you today?"
I always answer,
I always tell them,
If they ask me,
Politely. . . .
BUT SOMETIMES
  I wish
    That they wouldn't.

Jenny's father wants to teach her how to play tennis, but Jenny has different ideas. How does Jenny show her father what she really wants to do?

Jenny and the Tennis Nut

by Janet Schulman

Jenny stood on her hands. Just then her father came into the room. "Look at me. It is my best handstand yet," she said.

"What's so great about it?" asked her father.

She looked at him upside down and said, "I have been standing like this for a minute."

"Well, I have been standing like this for much longer," said her father. "Get yourself right side up. I have a surprise."

He gave her a long box. "It's a tennis racket," Jenny said.

"I'm going to teach you tennis and this will be your racket," he said.

Jenny picked up the racket. "What if I don't like tennis?" she asked.

"You're going to love tennis. I love tennis. Your mother does, and you will, too," said her father.

Her father picked up his racket and some tennis balls. "Come on outside, Jenny. We can hit the ball," he said.

He drew a line across the wall. "This line is the top of the net," he said.

"Some net. I can't jump over it when I win," said Jenny.

"First things first, Jenny. First learn to hit the ball. Like this," he said. Thonk went the ball. He hit the ball again and again. He loved hitting a tennis ball so much that he forgot about teaching Jenny.

Jenny did not mind. She was doing cartwheels on the grass.

At last he stopped. "Now you try," he said. He threw a ball to her. Swish went her racket. "Keep your eye on the ball, and you won't miss," he said. He threw another ball to her.

She kept her eye on the ball. Zing went the ball over the fence and into Mrs. Wister's yard.

"I'll get the ball," said Jenny. She took a running start and jumped up, up and over Mrs. Wister's fence.

"That was pretty good," said her father. Jenny smiled. "Oh, I can jump a lot higher than that," she said.

"I meant that you hit the ball pretty well," he said.

"Oh," she said. Jenny jumped back over the fence. "Then why did it go the wrong way into Mrs. Wister's yard?"

"Because you were facing the wall—I mean the net. Always stand with your side to the net," he said.

Jenny made a face.

"You will learn," he said. He threw a ball to her. She kept her eye on the ball. She stood with her side to the net. She swung the racket. Thonk went the ball.

"That's perfect!" said her father.

"Oh, Daddy, stop kidding," she said.

"Don't you want to be a great tennis player?" he asked.

"No. I want to be a great circus acrobat," she said.

"A circus acrobat! There are not many circuses looking for acrobats these days. You can play tennis anywhere. Think what fun we will have!" he said.

"You mean think what fun you will have," she said.

"Oh, Jenny," he said. "I just want you to have a sport you can do well and enjoy. That's why I want to teach you tennis."

She shook her head sadly. "Oh, Daddy, you have a one-track mind. Tennis, tennis, tennis," she said. "You are a tennis nut. I already have a sport I can do well, and I enjoy. Look!" She did four perfect cartwheels. Then she did a handstand and a flip.

Her father watched her. His eyes were wide open. "Hey, that's good. You are wonderful, Jenny."

Jenny ran to her father and threw her
arms around him. "You mean it's all
right for me to do my tricks?" she
asked.

"It's more than all right. I want you
to. I am going to put up some rings and
a bar with a nice soft mat under them,"
he said. "You do gymnastics well and
you really enjoy it. Gymnastics is right
for you."

"Just like tennis is right for you. Right?" she said.

"Right!" he answered. They were both happy.

Jenny looked up at her father. "There is something else, Daddy. Can I take gymnastics classes?"

Her father laughed. "You can read minds, too. Maybe you do belong in a circus," he said.

Jenny ran to the house. "I am going to tell Mom what my game is," she said.

Her father picked up his racket and a ball. There was no question what his game was.

In a few minutes Jenny came out again. She did a flip and watched her father hit the ball.

At last he stopped. "Maybe when you are older you will want a second game," he said. "I'll always be ready to teach you tennis when you are ready to learn."

"Okay," said Jenny. "If you ever want a second game, I'll always be ready to teach you cartwheels and flips. You would love it." She grinned at him, upside down.

1. How does Jenny show her father what she really wants to do?

2. Why doesn't Jenny want to learn how to play tennis?

3. How was the problem solved?

4. Where in the story did you first begin to think that Jenny would not have to learn to play tennis?

5. What did you think about the way Jenny showed her father what she wanted to do?

Think about something special that you have done for your parents. Write a paragraph about what you did and how your parents felt about it.

Everybody Says

by Dorothy Aldis

Everybody says
I look just like my mother.
Everybody says
I'm the image of Aunt Bee.
Everybody says
My nose is like my father's
But I want to look like ME!

This is a play about a duckling who is very different from the other ducklings. He does not like to be different. Does he change his mind?

The Ugly Duckling

A fairy tale retold by Frank Ruggiero

CHARACTERS

Hans Christian Andersen	**Ducklings**
Ugly Duckling	**Old Duck**
Mother Duck	**Children**
Mean Duck	**Swans**

Andersen: It is a beautiful spring day. In the meadow, Mother Duck is sitting on five eggs. They begin to hatch. The Old Duck from the duck yard has come to visit with Mother Duck.

Ducklings: Peep! Peep! How big the world is!

Mother Duck: I hope you are all hatched now. (stands up to look in her nest) No! There is still one more. It is the very biggest egg.

Old Duck: That last egg looks like a turkey egg. Leave it alone. Go teach your other ducklings to swim.

Mother Duck: I think I'll sit for a little longer.

Old Duck: Just as you please. (leaves)

Ugly Duckling: (begins to crack its shell) Peep! Peep!

Mother Duck: He is so big and gray! Can he really be a turkey chick? (turns to the other ducklings) Come, children, let's go to the pond to see if you can swim. (leads ducklings to the pond)

Ducklings: (in the pond) I can swim! I can swim!

Ugly Duckling: I like to swim!

Mother Duck: I'm so happy! All my ducklings can swim. The gray one is not a turkey! He swims very well.

Andersen: The next day, the ducklings followed Mother Duck to visit the duck yard. The duck yard was a loud place with many other ducks.

Mother Duck: This is the duck yard.

Mean Duck: (flying near the Ugly Duckling) He is so big and ugly. I am going to bite him.

Mother Duck: Leave him alone! He's not hurting anyone! (leads ducklings through the duck yard) Let's go visit with the others. Do you see that old duck? She is the greatest of them all. Bow your heads when you see her. Bend your necks and say "Quack!"

Ducklings: Quack! Quack!

Old Duck: You have fine ducklings, but the gray one is very ugly. He hasn't turned out well at all. I wish you could make him over again.

Mother Duck: It can't be done. He isn't pretty, but he swims well—even better than some of the others. He will grow to be strong. He will make his own way in the world.

Andersen: The other ducklings felt right at home. The Ugly Duckling was pushed and made fun of by the other ducklings and all the animals in the meadow. He was very sad.

Ugly Duckling: No one likes me. I'm so ugly. I think I'll fly away.

Andersen: The Ugly Duckling flew away. He stopped in a marsh where wild ducks lived. He stayed there for some time. After that, he flew to another pond. The leaves changed and fell from the trees. Winter came. It was very cold. The Ugly Duckling had to swim to keep from freezing. He felt sad. Days and weeks went by. Winter turned to spring. The Ugly Duckling wanted to see more of the world. He flew up over the edge of the pond. As he was flying, he spotted a lake.

Ugly Duckling: This is a pretty lake. I think I'll swim here for a while. (sees some birds) Those birds are so beautiful! They will make fun of me because I'm so ugly, but I would love to swim with them.

Andersen: As the Ugly Duckling flies down to the lake, he sees himself in the water. He can't believe his own eyes!

Ugly Duckling: I am no longer an Ugly Duckling! I am a beautiful swan!

Swans: (swimming around the Ugly Duckling) Come swim with us. You are such a wonderful swan! We have never seen a swan so beautiful!

Andersen: Every spring all the children waited for the swans to come back. The children would go down to the lake to feed bread to the swans.

Children: (laughing and dancing) There's a new swan this year! He is the most beautiful one of all!

Ugly Duckling: (holds his head high) I never dreamed I could be this happy when I was the Ugly Duckling!

1. Does the duckling change his mind? Why?

2. How did you feel about the Old Duck?

3. When did you first begin to think that the Ugly Duckling was not really a duckling?

4. How much time passed from the time the Ugly Duckling hatched until he knew he was a swan? How do you know?

**Think
and
Write**

Think about how you are different from everyone else and how that makes you special. Write a paragraph that tells what makes you a special person.

Caterpillars look very different from butterflies. How does a caterpillar change into a butterfly?

The Caterpillar's Surprise

by Grace Moremen

Some caterpillars turn into butterflies. Other caterpillars turn into moths. This is surprising because caterpillars look very different from butterflies or moths. Let's see how caterpillars turn into butterflies.

First, butterflies lay eggs on plants. The eggs are about as big as the head of a pin. Soon, caterpillars come out of the eggs. Little caterpillars look like tiny worms with many feet.

Some caterpillars have soft skin. Others have rough skin.

As a butterfly caterpillar grows, it becomes too big to fit inside its skin. So the old skin cracks open and falls off. Now the caterpillar has a new, bigger skin. The caterpillar will get a new skin three or four times while it is growing.

Butterfly caterpillars eat all day. Sometimes they eat all night, too. Caterpillars eat plants.

Some butterfly caterpillars will grow as long as a fingernail. Others will grow as big and fat as a crayon.

After a few weeks, the butterfly caterpillar stops eating. It finds a plant to hold on to and spins a covering around itself. The covering is called a *cocoon*. The caterpillar inside the cocoon is now called a *pupa*.

Inside the cocoon, the pupa is
changing. It is growing legs and wings
and a whole new body, but you cannot
see this happening. It is becoming a
butterfly.

Then one day the cocoon cracks open.
The butterfly pushes out its head. It
sticks up its two feelers. Then it wiggles
its body out of the cocoon. The new
butterfly stands up on its six thin legs.

The new butterfly is wet. Its wings are folded. Now the butterfly pumps liquid into its wings. This liquid helps the butterfly to open them. Then the butterfly dries its wings by flapping them. You can see how different the butterfly looks from the caterpillar.

A butterfly lays eggs. A baby caterpillar comes out of each egg. The caterpillar spins a cocoon and turns into a pupa. Then the pupa turns into a butterfly. This is the caterpillar's wonderful surprise.

Discuss the Selection

1. How does a caterpillar become a butterfly?

2. How does the butterfly open and dry its wings?

3. What did you learn that was a surprise to you?

4. Where on page 190 did you know about the caterpillar's surprise?

Think and Write

Think about a butterfly coming out of its cocoon near your house. Write a paragraph to tell the caterpillar all about its new home.

Follow Directions

Make a Paper Caterpillar

You have just learned how a caterpillar turns into a butterfly. Now you can make a caterpillar to play with.

To make your caterpillar, you must follow the directions carefully. Here are some things to remember about following directions.

1. Get all the things you need together before you begin.
2. Read the steps very carefully.
3. Begin with step 1 and follow all the steps in order.
4. Do not leave out any steps.

Paper Chain Caterpillars

Things you will need:

a ruler

scissors

1 sheet of yellow paper

1 sheet of green paper

paste

crayons

string

a pencil

1. With a pencil and ruler, draw four 2-inch strips on the yellow paper.

Cut along the lines. Do the same with the green paper.

2.

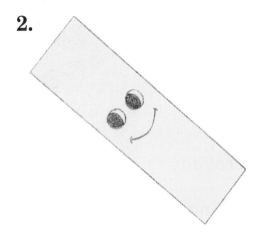

2. With a crayon, draw big eyes and a mouth on one yellow strip.

3. On one green strip, draw two feelers.

3.

4. Cut out the feelers. Paste them just over the eyes. Fold them so they stand straight up.

4.

5. Take the head and make it into a circle. Paste the ends together.

5.

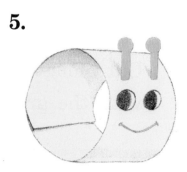

6. Now take a green strip and make it into a circle through the head of the caterpillar. You are making a paper chain.

6.

7. Keep doing this until you have used all the strips. Your caterpillar is finished.

7.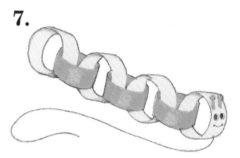

You may want to draw stripes or spots on your caterpillar. You can also tie a string to its head. Pull the string, and the caterpillar will follow you wherever you go!

Thinking About "Kaleidoscopes"

In "Kaleidoscopes," you read about many interesting changes. You found out that the prince really liked life in his castle better than working hard on a farm. The Ugly Duckling found out he had always been a beautiful swan. You learned how a caterpillar changed into a beautiful butterfly. Beatrice changed the way she felt about the library. Jenny's father let her do gymnastics because she didn't like tennis.

Some of the characters found that things are not always what they seem to be. What are some other changes that took place in the stories? What things didn't change? As you read other stories, watch to see how people and things can change.

1. How are Beatrice and the prince in "The Simple Prince" alike?

2. How are Jenny and Beatrice alike?

3. Why do you think "Tell Me a Story" comes right after "Beatrice Doesn't Want To"?

4. How are the Ugly Duckling and caterpillars alike?

Unit 4

Scrapbooks

A scrapbook is a book into which you put things that you would like to remember. In "Scrapbooks," you will read about some people who have made scrapbooks. You will also read about some special days that are fun to remember. See how people all over the world greet the new year. Read an old, old tale that has been told for many years about a small town.

As you read "Scrapbooks," think about the special times that the people in each story like to remember. What makes these times special?

Birdie Blue

Candy Apple

Local Class Visits City Zoo

FIELD TRIP HUGE SUCCESS

Local Class Visits City

Read on Your Own

The Patchwork Cat *by Nicola Bayley and William Mayne. Knopf.* Tabby the cat finds herself far from home after she is carried away with the garbage.

Abby *by Jeannette Caines. Harper.* Abby loves to look at her baby book. It starts with her adoption.

Happy Birthday! *by Gail Gibbons. Holiday.* This book tells about the history, fun, and folklore of birthdays.

Up North in Winter *by Deborah Hartley. Dutton.* Grandpa Ole tells how he saved a fox and then lost it on a freezing night long ago.

Katie Morag and the Two Grandmothers *by Mairi Hedderwick. Little, Brown.* Katie's two grandmothers are very different and do not get along well. A special time brings them together.

At Grandma and Grandpa's House *by Ruth Hooker. Whitman.* A little boy tells of the wonderful times he has at his grandparents' house.

Jafta's Father *by Hugh Lewin. Carolrhoda.* A South African boy tells of the wonderful times he has when his father is home with the family..

When I Was Nine *by James Stevenson. Greenwillow.* A grown-up tells of a trip the family took out west on a vacation when he was nine years old.

*This is a story about a boy who keeps
a scrapbook for his grandmother.
What does he put into the scrapbook?*

Grandma Without Me

story and pictures by Judith Vigna

I don't want Thanksgiving this year.
It won't be any fun without Grandma.
Grandma is Dad's mother. She lives far
away, in another town.

I don't see why we can't visit Grandma for Thanksgiving. We have to stay home because Mom says things are different now. Mom and Dad don't live together anymore. Mom says I can visit Dad's new house whenever I want. That's great, but I want to visit Grandma's house again. I like my room there and the way Grandma fixes pancakes for me.

We've never had Thanksgiving without Grandma. She always cooked a huge turkey, and Mom and Dad and I put on funny hats. One time I ate so much turkey I got sick. It was the best day of my life.

Now, Grandma and I write to each other all the time. A while ago, Grandma sent me a scrapbook and a letter. The letter said:

My darling boy,
Your mom doesn't want to visit me right now. Things will get better. It will just take time. One day we'll see each other again. I am sending a scrapbook for you to keep for us. Until we see each other again, we'll keep in touch through your scrapbook. I will always love you.
Grandma

· The letter was the first thing I put into my scrapbook.

Grandma and I work on my scrapbook a lot. I saved a purple leaf that I found, and I put it into the scrapbook.

I put some other things into my scrapbook. Grandma sent me a feather from her bird's cage.

I took a picture of the new bike Dad got me for my birthday.

Grandma sent me a funny picture she saw in the newspaper.

This morning I got a mailgram! It said:

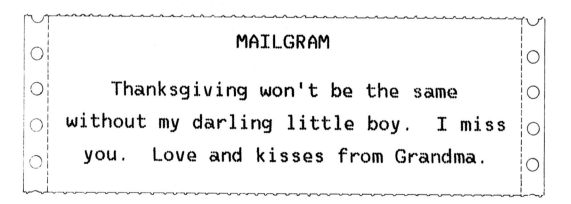

MAILGRAM

Thanksgiving won't be the same without my darling little boy. I miss you. Love and kisses from Grandma.

It was neat of Grandma to send me a real mailgram for my scrapbook. Grandma must really miss me! I think I'll send her something special, so she won't feel so bad.

I asked Mom for a really big sheet of paper. Then I asked her to help me. I told her that I wanted to lie down on the paper. She could draw around me. Then I could send the picture to Grandma. Grandma will feel like I'm at her house for Thanksgiving after all!

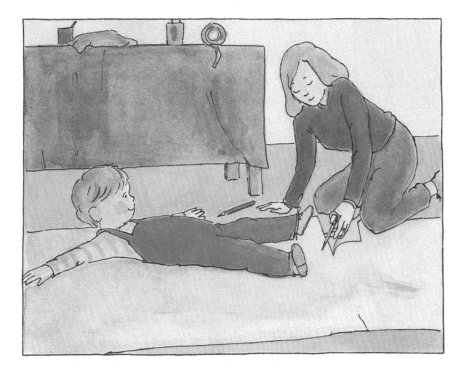

Mom has promised we can really go to visit Grandma next Thanksgiving.

1. What does the boy put into his scrapbook?

2. Do you think the scrapbook was a good idea? Why?

3. How did the boy solve his problem of not going to his grandmother's for Thanksgiving?

4. Why do you think the boy's mother said they would visit his grandmother next year?

5. What words in the story tell you the boy wants to do something special for his grandma?

**Think
and
Write**

Think about someone you would like to invite to your house for Thanksgiving. Write an invitation.

Keepsakes

by Leland B. Jacobs

I keep bottle caps,
 I keep strings,
I keep keys and corks
 And all such things.

When people say,
"What good are they?"
The answer's hard to get
For just how I will use them all
I don't know yet.

Summarize

When you tell about a story you have
read, you give a summary. You do not
tell all of the words the author uses,
but you give the important details.
When you tell what the author's story
was about, you **summarize**.

Read the following summary of
"Grandma Without Me."

The boy and his grandma didn't
see each other this Thanksgiving.
So they used a scrapbook to keep
in touch. The boy put things he
wanted his grandma to know
about into his scrapbook. He also
sent something special so she
would feel as if they were
together.

The summary you just read was a good one. How can you tell? It tells all the important details from the story.

Now read the following summary of "The Ugly Duckling."

> Mother Duck had some ducklings. One duckling was different from the others. This one flew away.

Is this a good summary? Why? It is not a very good summary because it does not tell all the important details from the story. What details should be in this summary? The duckling was big and ugly, and the other ducklings made fun of him. He flew away, and he lived alone all winter. In the spring, he found out he was a beautiful swan.

A summary must have the important details from a story. Summarizing a story can help you better understand and remember what you read.

Making a scrapbook can be a lot of fun. What kinds of things can you put into a scrapbook?

Scrapbooks

by Alma Marshak Whitney

Have you ever thought of making a scrapbook? You can make a scrapbook about anything you want. The first thing you need is a book with blank pages. The book becomes a scrapbook when you start to put things into it.

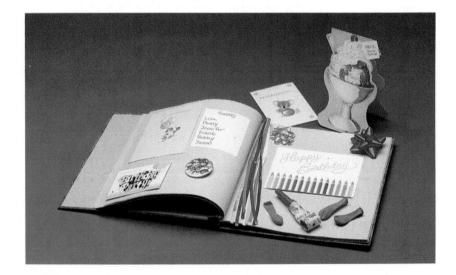

Lisa Bates, Jason Cook, and Terry Parks are making scrapbooks. Lisa is making a scrapbook with pictures she collects. The name of her scrapbook is *The Lions*. The pictures are of the players on the Lions baseball team.

Lisa looks through newspapers for pictures of her favorite players on the Lions. Lisa cuts out the pictures she finds. Then she pastes these pictures into her scrapbook. Sometimes Lisa gets baseball cards with pictures of her favorite players on them. Lisa puts these cards into her scrapbook, too.

Terry is making a scrapbook about the birthday party she had a few weeks ago. The name of her scrapbook is *My Favorite Birthday*.

Terry has put many things into her scrapbook. There is a list of her friends who came to the party. There is a list of the games they played. There is a balloon Terry let the air out of when the party was over. There are also the birthday cards Terry got from her friends at the party.

Terry is glad that she is making this scrapbook. She thinks it will help her remember how nice her birthday party was.

Jason is making a scrapbook he calls *My Book of Trips*. He plans to put into it things he collects from trips he takes.

Jason started making the scrapbook after he came home from visiting with his Aunt Betty and Uncle Mike. There is a ticket to a movie Jason saw with his aunt and uncle. There is a picture from a place where he ate lunch with them one day. There is a page from a newspaper that people read in the town where Aunt Betty and Uncle Mike live. There are cards with pictures of buildings Jason saw in the town. Jason even saved his airplane ticket to put into his scrapbook.

Jason likes to look at his scrapbook. It helps him remember what a good time he had on his trip. He wants to collect things from other trips. Then his scrapbook will help him remember the good times he has had on many trips.

Perhaps you might like to make a scrapbook. You can make a scrapbook about many different things. The things you put into your scrapbook will make it special to you.

1. What kinds of things can be put into a scrapbook?

2. Why do people keep scrapbooks?

3. Which scrapbook in the story did you like best? Why?

4. What words in the story tell why Terry keeps a scrapbook?

5. If you were to make a scrapbook, what kinds of things would you put into it?

Think and Write

Think about what you would want people to know about you. Write a story that tells what you look like, what you like to do, and some of your favorite things.

Wei Chou's family is getting ready for a special celebration. What does Wei Chou do to make the celebration really special?

The Year of the Smile

by John Yeates

Wei Chou was very happy today. It was the first day of the Chinese New Year. This morning Wei Chou's parents gave her a red envelope. There was money inside. It was a New Year's gift.

Wei Chou's real name was Susie. One day her father called her Wei Chou— which means "a smile" in Chinese. Wei Chou liked both names, but most of the time she used her Chinese name.

Wei Chou and her mother were making the house pretty. Over each doorway they placed a long, red silk ribbon. In each window they hung a red paper lantern. Wei Chou even tied a red ribbon around her puppy's neck.

"Red makes me happy," said Wei Chou.

"Good," said her mother. "Many things make you happy. That is why your father named you Wei Chou."

Wei Chou went into her room and hung the last lantern over her puppy's bed. Then she sat down near the puppy.

She thought of all the good things about the New Year's celebration. It was a happy time for the family. They got new clothes. They ate special foods. Wei Chou liked the Eight Treasure Dessert. Her mother and father made it every year. Sometimes they let her help.

Suddenly the puppy jumped from his
bed. He ran to the front door. Wei Chou
followed him. Her mother went to the
door, too.

"Why is the puppy barking so much?"
asked Wei Chou.

"He may know that we have a surprise
for you," said her mother. "I think I
hear the surprise now."

The front door opened. Wei Chou's
father came in. Someone was with him.

"It's Uncle Li!" shouted Wei Chou, as
she ran to meet him.

Uncle Li handed Wei Chou a box.
When she opened it, she saw a
beautiful doll. It was dressed in a
Chinese costume. Wei Chou hugged her
uncle and thanked him for the doll.

He said, "It was a long ride on the
bus, but I wanted to help with the
celebration. What time does the parade
begin this afternoon?"

"We will not have a parade," said
Wei Chou's father.

Uncle Li shook his head. He looked
very sad. "No parade?" he asked.

"Not this year," said Wei Chou's
father. "Mr. Wu always made plans for
our parade, but he moved away."

Uncle Li did not smile for the rest of the morning. He did not smile at lunch. "No parade," he said again and again.

Wei Chou wished that Uncle Li would smile. That afternoon she had an idea.

She rode her bike to Amy's house. "Meet me at the picnic table in the park," Wei Chou said. "Bring everyone you can find. Tell them to bring their New Year's costumes. Tell Timmie to bring his drum, too."

Wei Chou went back to her house. She found some crayons, some colored paper, and some scissors. She put them all into a big paper bag with her costume. Then she ran out the front door.

Her friends were waiting in the park. "Let's have a parade," she said to them. "Let's put on our costumes. We can be a dragon. I will make the mask."

She drew a dragon's head on the paper bag with her crayons. Then she cut two small holes for the eyes. She made a large hole for the mouth. Wei Chou's friends made little flags from the colored paper.

"We are ready," said Wei Chou.

The children made a line. Wei Chou put on the mask. Amy was the last in line. She was the dragon's tail.

Timmie began to play his drum. The children waved their flags. The dragon moved forward down the sidewalk. People came out of their houses to see it.

Officer Butler saw the dragon. "Where is this snake going?" he asked.

"This is not a snake," said Wei Chou. "This is a dragon. We are having a New Year's parade."

"Then I will lead the parade," Officer Butler said.

Uncle Li and Wei Chou's parents were standing in the yard. The puppy was sitting in the grass. They saw the dragon and the children in their costumes.

Uncle Li was smiling. He ran to meet them. "Now all we need are some fireworks," he said.

Wei Chou's puppy ran after the dragon. He barked loudly.

Uncle Li turned around. "We do not need anything now," he said. "That puppy sounds enough like fireworks!"

Wei Chou laughed and said, "Shin Nee-an Kie Lo," which means "Happy New Year."

"You have made me very happy," said Uncle Li. "Each Chinese year has a name. This is the Year of the Dragon, but I will call it the Year of the Smile."

1. What did Wei Chou do to make the celebration special?

2. When did you first begin to know what Wei Chou was going to do for her uncle?

3. Do you think Wei Chou was a good name for the girl in the story?

4. How did Wei Chou make Uncle Li happy?

Think and Write

Think about your favorite special day. Make a poster that tells about your special day. On another sheet of paper, write why your day is special and tell what you do.

How do people in different countries make the first day of a new year a day to remember?

New Year's Day

by Martha and Charles Shapp

People all over the world celebrate the beginning of a new year. Most people celebrate the first of January as New Year's Day.

Other people celebrate New Year's Day at different times of the year. In some countries New Year's Day is celebrated in the spring when the flowers begin to bloom. All people do not celebrate New Year's Day at the same time, but they all celebrate the beginning of the new year in some way.

The celebration often starts on New Year's Eve. This is the last night of the old year.

On New Year's Eve, many people celebrate by having parties at home. At midnight the old year ends, and the new year begins. People shake hands or kiss, and everybody shouts, "Happy New Year!"

Some people meet in the streets to bring in the new year. They laugh and sing and blow horns. In some cities, people in the street join hands and sing "Auld Lang Syne" at midnight.

In parts of Africa, people greet the new year with dances. The children of Scotland have lots of fun on New Year's Eve. They go from house to house and sing songs. The people of Mexico celebrate the new year with a big fiesta, or party.

In some countries, people open their doors wide just before midnight on New Year's Eve. They do this to let the old year out and the new year in.

Some people believe that they must make a "clean start" for the new year. They give their homes a good cleaning before the new year comes. Other people make a clean start by pouring clean water on their heads.

Some people get ready for the new year by throwing away their old dishes. They get new dishes for the new year.

Chinese people all over the world celebrate New Year's Day with parades. The Chinese New Year's Day comes in February. A big, make-believe dragon has an important part in this parade.

Parades are also held in cities all across the United States. In one city, people dress up in funny costumes. Then they parade through the streets.

Roses grow in California in January. So, a city in California celebrates with a Parade of Roses.

Different people celebrate New Year's Day at different times and in different ways. However, all around the world, people celebrate the beginning of a new year.

1. How do people make New Year's Day a day to remember?

2. What do most people do on New Year's Day?

3. What did you think when you read that some people throw out their dishes to celebrate the new year?

4. Where did you read what children in Scotland do on New Year's Eve?

5. Name two ways that people celebrate the beginning of a new year.

Think and Write

Think about how you might make a "clean start" at the beginning of a year. Write about some things you wish you could do better.

The New Year

by Jane W. Krows

A brand New Year arrived last night;
It came while I was waiting.
But I did not hear the horns or shouts
Of people celebrating.
Because, you see, I fell asleep
Before the hour, when
The old year silently passed out
And the New Year entered in.
But I have a clean new calendar
Which hangs before my eyes
And every day that's listed
Will hold a new surprise.

Story Elements

There are many different things that make up a story. In most stories, you read about the characters and the things that happen to these characters.

Many things happen in a story, but there is only one main **problem.** The problem in "The Year of the Smile" was that Uncle Li was unhappy because there was not going to be a parade for the Chinese New Year. When you find the problem in a story, you can start to think about how some of the characters might try to solve it.

Wei Chou did not want Uncle Li to be unhappy, so she planned a parade. What Wei Chou did to solve the problem is called the **solution.**

Read the following sentences about "Grandma Without Me." Tell which is the main problem in the story.

1. The boy kept a scrapbook.
2. The boy and his grandma could not see each other for Thanksgiving.
3. The boy put a picture of his new bike in his scrapbook.

Which sentence tells what the problem is? Sentence 2 tells the problem.

Now read the following sentences. Tell which is the solution to the problem.

1. The boy and his grandma used a scrapbook to keep in touch.
2. The boy saved a leaf in his scrapbook.
3. His grandma sent him a mailgram.

If you said sentence 1, you read carefully.
Look for problems and solutions as you read. Once you can tell what the problem is in a story, you can look for details that tell how it will be solved.

This is a very old story about a small town in the state of Delaware. People who live in the town now are still telling this story. What happened to the town?

Cornstalks and Cannonballs

by Barbara Mitchell

Long ago there was a little town by the sea. It was called Lewes (LOO-iss). Lewes was a pretty town. Fishing boats filled the bay. Sea birds flew. Sea winds blew.

Lewes was a nice town. Fishermen got up before the sun to go fishing. Farmers worked hard in their fields. All the people were very happy in their little town.

One winter day, the fishermen came home with some bad news. English ships were in the bay. There were many cannons on these ships. England and the United States were fighting again!

The English would not let any other
ships into Delaware Bay. They also would
not let any boats out. The fishermen
could not work. All day they sat and
talked and worried and wondered.
Everyone watched and waited. They
waited for a very long time.

The sailors on the ships didn't have much food left. They told one of their captains, "Sir John, we want meat! We want vegetables! We want to eat!"

So Sir John sat down and wrote a note.

To the people of Lewes, Delaware:

Send us meat, Send us vegetables. If you don't, we will fire on your town.

Sir John thought that the little town would be afraid. "Soon we will be eating meat and vegetables," he told his sailors.

The people of Lewes were not afraid. They were angry. "Send you our meat and vegetables?" they said. "Never! We will never feed you!"

When Sir John did not get the food, he could not believe it! He wondered what to do next.

The people of Lewes did not sit still. "We will fight!" they said. "Sam Davis will be our captain."

"Let's clean up the old cannons!" someone said. They cleaned up four old cannons. Then the little town waited in the dark. The English didn't fire on the town.

A few weeks later, Sir John's sailors were just about out of food. "Where is our meat? Where are our vegetables?" they shouted. So Sir John sent another note to the town.

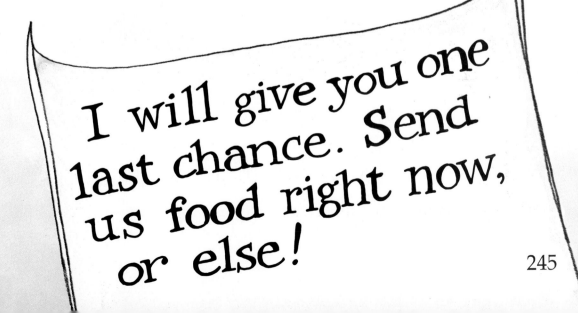

I will give you one last chance. Send us food right now, or else!

The people of the town still did not send food to the sailors. Sir John was even more angry now. "Ready! Fire!" he shouted.

Cannonballs flew at the little town. The English fired fast. The people of Lewes did not fire as fast. They did not have many cannonballs.

Then the people of Lewes fired their last cannonball. The farmers looked at the fishermen. The fishermen looked at the farmers. They all looked at the beach. It was covered with cannonballs that the English had just fired. Sam Davis said, "Let me see one of those cannonballs."

He took the ball to a cannon. The ball went right in. The English cannonballs fit the town cannons!

"Call out the boys!" Sam Davis shouted. They all came running. He told them to get the cannonballs on the beach and carry them to the cannons. Then the people of Lewes fired the cannonballs back at the English ships.

Sam Davis was still worried. He knew his little town was not as strong as the English ships. He looked at the farmers' fields. He saw dry cornstalks coming up through the snow. Suddenly he smiled.

Then he shouted to the farmers, "Bring me those cornstalks! Bring me your farm tools! We are going to make a fire!"

"Farm tools?" asked the farmers. They did as they were told.

While the farmers were gone, Sam Davis made a fire. When the farmers came back, he took a hoe. He held the hoe close to the fire. He held it just close enough to make it black.

"Make all the tools and cornstalks black," Sam told the men.

That night, Sir John said, "The town is out of cannonballs. Get out the rowboats. We will row to the beach and take over."

"Look, Sir!" shouted a sailor. People were filling the town. They came down the streets and across the beaches.

They were the people of the little town. Some of them were women dressed as men. In the dark, Sir John could not tell the men from the women. It looked as if they all carried guns. Those guns were really just cornstalks and hoes and sticks and brooms that had been made black.

"Look at all the people! They have guns!" shouted a sailor.

"There are too many people for us to fight! Go back to the ships!" Sir John yelled.

So the English sailors went back to their ships. They sailed away. They never came back.

The fishermen went back to their fishing. The farmers picked up their tools and went back to their farms.

The sea birds flew and the sea winds blew in that brave little town of long ago.

1. What happened to Lewes, Delaware?

2. What made the people of Lewes very angry?

3. What did you think of Sam Davis's plan to fool the English?

4. Name two ways the people of Lewes worked together to solve their problems.

5. What did you read that tells you how the women helped? Find that part of the story.

**Think
and
Write**

Think about what might have happened if the people of Lewes did not think of a way to fool the English. Write a new ending to the story.

This is the story of an old quilt. What are some of the things that happened to the quilt?

The Quilt Story

by Tony Johnston

Long ago, a little girl's mother made a quilt to keep the girl warm when the snow came down. The mother sewed the quilt by a yellow flame. As she sewed, she hummed. She stitched the tails of falling stars on the quilt. She also stitched the name Abigail on it.

Abigail loved the quilt. She wrapped it around her in the quiet dark and watched the winter skies.

Sometimes Abigail played in the woods near her home. She had milk. Her dolls had milk. The quilt had milk all over it.

Sometimes Abigail pretended the quilt was a gown. She put it on when she pretended to ride her horse to town. The quilt ripped. So her mother fixed it.

When Abigail played hide-and-seek with her sisters, she hid under the quilt. She was quiet, but her sisters still found her.

Abigail slept under the quilt when she was sick. It kept her warm.

One day Abigail's family moved away, across wide rivers and over a rock-hard trail. The quilt went too. It was not stuffed into the trunks. It kept Abigail and her sisters warm from the wild winds. It kept them warm from the rain and the cold nights.

Abigail's father built a new house in the woods. He built Abigail a new bed. He made her a new wooden horse, too. When Abigail's father was finished, everyone said, "Welcome home."

Abigail felt sad. They had a new house, a new horse, and a new bed. Everything was new, except the quilt. So Abigail's mother rocked her as mothers do. Then she tucked her in, and Abigail felt at home again under the quilt.

One day when the quilt was very old and very loved, Abigail folded it carefully and put it in the attic. Many years passed. Everyone forgot the quilt was in the attic.

A raccoon came and loved the quilt. It dug a hole in it with its black paws. The raccoon hid some food there.

A cat came and loved the quilt. It rolled on the stars, and the stuffing spilled out like snow. Then the cat rolled up in the snow and purred.

"Kitty, Kitty," called a little girl. She found her cat, and she found the quilt. The little girl wrapped the quilt around her. She loved it, too.

"Can you make it like new?" she asked
her mother. So her mother fixed the holes.
She pushed fresh stuffing into the quilt. She
stitched long tails on the stars to swish
across the quilt again.

One day the little girl's family moved
miles and miles away.

Her family found a new house. It was freshly cleaned and freshly painted. The family unpacked and unpacked all night. When they were finished, everyone said, "Welcome home."

The little girl felt sad. Everything was new, except the quilt. So the little girl's mother rocked her as mothers do. Then she tucked her in, and the little girl felt at home again under the quilt.

1. What things happened to the quilt?

2. How did the little girls and the animals feel about the quilt? Why?

3. Why did the little girls feel at home under the quilt?

4. How did you feel when the raccoon made a hole in the quilt? Why?

5. Where in the story did you know how the second little girl felt about the quilt?

Think and Write

Pretend you are going to move to a new place. Write a story about something you would take to help you feel at home.

Arthur is selling all of his old toys. There is one toy that is very special to him. Who buys that toy? How does Arthur feel after it is sold?

Arthur's Honey Bear

story and pictures by Lillian Hoban

It was spring-cleaning day. Violet was cleaning out her toy chest. She made two piles of toys — one to keep, and one to put away. Arthur was sticking stamps into his stamp book.

"I am going to clean out my toy chest, too," said Arthur. "Then I am going to have a Tag Sale."

"What is a Tag Sale?" asked Violet.

"A Tag Sale is a sale you have to sell your old junk," said Arthur.

"I don't have any old junk," said Violet. "I want to keep all of my toys."

"When I was little," said Arthur, "I wanted to keep all of my toys, too. Now I want to sell some of them." Arthur began to clean out his toy chest. He took a pile of toys to the back steps.

Arthur took his Hula-Hoop, his Yo-Yo, and a pile of finger paintings. He took Noah's Ark, his baby King Kong, his sandbox set, his Old Maid cards, and his rocks and marbles. Then he took out his Honey Bear.

"Father gave me Honey Bear when I had the chicken pox," said Arthur. "Honey Bear always tasted my medicine for me when I was sick." Arthur moved Honey Bear behind baby King Kong.

"Now I will make the price tags," said Arthur.

"Let me help," said Violet.

"You can cut the paper for the tags," said Arthur, "and I will write the prices."

Arthur made a big sign. It said:

Then Arthur marked the prices on the tags. He put tags on all the toys and pictures and rocks and marbles.

"You didn't put a tag on Honey Bear," said Violet.

"He is in very good shape," said Arthur. "He has only one eye missing. Maybe I should sell him for a lot of money. Maybe I should sell him for thirty-one cents."

"His ear is falling off," said Violet.

"Well," said Arthur, "I have not made up my mind yet." He moved Honey Bear all the way behind baby King Kong.

"Now," said Arthur, "we have to make arrows. Then everyone will know where the sale is."

Violet cut arrow shapes out of paper. Arthur wrote "Tag Sale" on them.

Arthur and Violet hung the arrows on trees. "Now we will wait for someone to come and buy," said Arthur. They waited and waited.

"Here comes Wilma. Maybe she will buy something," said Violet.

"Friday is my sister's birthday," said
Wilma. "Do you have anything good?"

"Well," said Arthur, "here is a very nice
Hula-Hoop."

"It's bent," said Wilma, "and my sister
has a Hula-Hoop. How much is the bear?"

"What bear?" asked Arthur.

"The bear behind baby King Kong," said
Wilma. "He doesn't have a price tag."

"Oh," said Arthur quickly, "he costs a lot."

"Well, how much?" asked Wilma.

"Your sister won't like him," said Arthur. "She is too old for stuffed toys."

"No, she isn't," said Wilma. "She takes her stuffed pig to bed with her."

"Well," said Arthur, "I will sell him to you for fifty cents."

"All right," said Wilma. She took fifty cents out of her pocket.

"Do you gift wrap?" asked Wilma.

"No," said Arthur.

"Well," said Wilma, "I don't have money for wrapping paper. If I buy a present at the toy store, they will gift wrap for nothing." Wilma put the fifty cents back in her pocket and walked away.

Arthur looked at Honey Bear and hugged him. He held Honey Bear.

"I wish someone would buy *something*," said Arthur.

Violet said, "I will buy something, Arthur. I will buy your Honey Bear."

"You don't have any money," said Arthur.

"I have thirty-one cents," said Violet. "I can give you thirty-one cents and my brand-new Color-Me-Nice coloring book. None of the pictures are colored in yet."

"Well, maybe," said Arthur, "but maybe I want to keep Honey Bear for myself."

"I thought you said you don't want to keep your old junk," said Violet.

"Honey Bear is not old junk," said Arthur. "He is my special bear."

"I will give you thirty-one cents, my Color-Me-Nice coloring book, and my box of crayons," said Violet. "Only the purple one is broken."

"Honey Bear has been my bear for a long time," said Arthur. "He wants me to take care of him."

"I will give you thirty-one cents, my coloring book, my crayons, and the prize from the box of cereal we ate this morning," said Violet.

"Well, all right," said Arthur. So Violet
gave Arthur thirty-one cents, her crayons,
her coloring book, and the prize from the
box of cereal. Arthur gave Violet his Honey
Bear.

Arthur took all of his sale things and put
them away. He put the thirty-one cents in
his mailbox bank. Then he colored a picture
in his Color-Me-Nice coloring book. He
colored a picture of a boy holding a bear.

Violet came in holding Honey Bear. He
was dressed in a pink tutu. He was wearing
a necklace and a hat.

"Honey Bear is a *boy*!" said Arthur. "He does not like those clothes."

"Honey Bear is my bear now," said Violet. "I will dress him the way I want."

"You don't know how to take care of him," said Arthur.

"Well, I am his mother now," said Violet, "and I am taking care of him."

"I think Honey Bear misses me," said Arthur. "He wishes he were still *my* bear."

"Well, he's not," said Violet. She took Honey Bear for a walk.

Arthur sat down and opened the Color-Me-Nice coloring book again. Then he hummed a little tune, and thought for a while. Violet came back. She sat down with Honey Bear. Arthur thought some more. Then he said to Violet, "Violet, are you my little sister?"

"Yes," said Violet.

"Well then, do you know what I am?" asked Arthur.

"You are my big brother," said Violet.

"Yes, I am," said Arthur, "and do you know what that means?"

"No," said Violet.

"That means I am Honey Bear's *uncle*!" said Arthur. Arthur picked up Honey Bear and hugged him. "I am your uncle, Honey Bear," said Arthur. "I will always be your uncle. Do you know what uncles do?" said Arthur to Honey Bear.

"What do uncles do?" asked Violet.

"Uncles play with their nephews, and take them out for treats," said Arthur.

"Honey Bear likes treats," said Violet. "Can I come, too?"

"All right," said Arthur.

Arthur took the thirty-one cents out of his mailbox bank. Then he and Violet and Honey Bear went out for a treat.

Honey Bear sat on his Uncle Arthur's lap. "Honey Bear, I am glad I will always be your uncle," said Arthur.

1. Who bought Arthur's Honey Bear?

2. How did Arthur feel after he sold Honey Bear? Why?

3. What did you think about Arthur selling Honey Bear?

4. How did Arthur get over missing Honey Bear?

5. When did you first think that Arthur did not want to sell Honey Bear?

6. Arthur was really too old to keep Honey Bear. How did he find a way to keep Honey Bear anyway?

Thinking About "Scrapbooks"

In "Scrapbooks," you read about special celebrations and things that are fun to remember. You found out some things that people like to put into scrapbooks. You learned about how people all over the world celebrate the beginning of a new year. You read about how the people of Lewes, Delaware, saved their town. You followed the story of a quilt that was passed from one family to another.

As you read other stories, look for the special times people want to remember. What do the people do to remember these times?

1. How did the boy in "Grandma Without Me" and Wei Chou make someone in their families happy?

2. What special day might the people of Lewes, Delaware, celebrate? How might they celebrate?

3. How is Abigail's quilt like a scrapbook?

4. Who do you think Arthur might ask to his New Year's celebration? Why?

Glossary*

The glossary is a special dictionary for this book. To find a word, use alphabetical, or ABC, order. For example, to find the word *swing* in the glossary, first look for the part of the glossary that has words beginning with the letter *s*. Then use the guide words to help you find the entry word *swing*. The glossary gives the meaning of the word as it is used in the book. Then the word is used in a sentence.

Sometimes different forms of the word follow the sentence. If a different form of the word, such as *swung*, is used in the book, then that word is used in the sentence.

Synonyms are included after some entries. This is shown as *syn.* if one synonym is given or *syns.* if more than one is given.

A blue box ■ at the end of the entry means that there is a picture to go with that word.

*Adapted entries that appear on the following pages are reprinted from *HBJ School Dictionary,* copyright © 1985 by Harcourt Brace Jovanovich, Inc. Reprinted by permission of Harcourt Brace Jovanovich, Inc.

A

alone Without anything or anyone: Please leave the dog *alone*.

along With or beside: Come *along* with me. *syn.* with

angry Feeling mad: Leah felt *angry* when Adam broke her toy. *syn.* mad

arrow A sign used to point the way: These *arrows* point to my house. **arrows** *syn.* pointer

attic The part of a house just under the roof: The large boxes were in the *attic*. **attics**

B

baby A child when it is very young: The *baby* is two weeks old. **babies** *syn.* infant

beautiful Very pretty: This is a *beautiful* dress. *syns.* pretty, good-looking

because The reason why: I can't go outside *because* I am sick. *syn.* since

become To turn into something: Yellow *becomes* green when blue is added. **became, becoming**

belong To be part of: The toy dog *belongs* to Lisa. **belongs, belonging**

bend To become curved in shape: *Bend* the piece of clay to form a circle. **bent, bending** *syn.* curve

bifocals Glasses with which people can see things that are near and things that are far away: His *bifocals* let him look up from his book and watch for the mail carrier. ■

body The main part of a person or animal, not including arms, head, and legs: The frog has a small *body* and long back legs. **bodies**

bow The bending of the head or body in greeting: He took a *bow* when he finished singing. **bows** *syn.* nod ■

broken Not working; in pieces: That toy is *broken*.

brook A waterway smaller than a river: He could catch many fish in the *brook*. **brooks** *syn.* stream

brother A boy who has the same parents as another person: My *brother* is the oldest in the family. **brothers**

build To put things together in order to make something: The people *built* the barn. **built, building** *syns.* make, create

butter The thick, yellowish fat that separates from milk or cream as it is churned: She put *butter* on her beans. ■

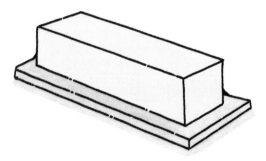

buy To pay money to get something: She will *buy* a book at the store. **bought, buying** *syn.* purchase

C

cage   A box-like pen for an animal: He just cleaned his rabbit's *cage*. **cages** *syns.* pen, coop

cannon   A large gun: The old *cannons* were used long ago. **cannons**

cannonball   A large, metal ball shot from a cannon: The *cannonballs* were loaded into the cannons. **cannonballs**

caterpillar   The wormlike body of some insects, such as the butterfly or moth, after they hatch from the egg: Those *caterpillars* are eating the leaves. **caterpillars** ■

celebrate   To have or join in a party to honor a special day or event: We *celebrate* my birthday every year. **celebrated, celebrating**

celebration   A party in honor of a special day or event: They had a big *celebration* after they won the game. **celebrations** *syns.* fiesta, festival

cent   A penny: She gave him ten *cents* for the book. **cents** *syn.* penny

cereal   A grain often made into breakfast food: This *cereal* is good for you. **cereals** *syns.* mush, porridge ■

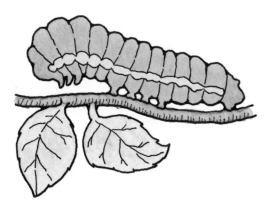

chick A young bird: The mother hen is looking for her little *chick*. **chicks** ■

churn To mix or stir very hard: We will *churn* the cream to make butter. **churned, churning** *syns.* mix, stir ■

circle A ring shape: They stand in a *circle* to play the game. **circles** *syns.* ring, loop

city A very large town: Big *cities* have many tall buildings. **cities**

class A school group that learns together: Miriam is in our *class*. **classes** *syns.* group, grade

clear Easy to see: This picture is very *clear.*

clothes Things to wear: He has some new school *clothes. syn.* wardrobe

clue A hint: She gave me a *clue* to help me find the book. **clues** *syns.* hint, tip

cocoon A covering for a caterpillar: This *cocoon* shows us that one day there will be a butterfly. **cocoons** ■

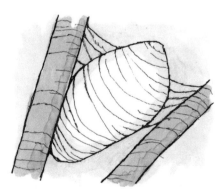

collect To bring things together: Selena *collects* stories from her grandparents. **collected, collecting** *syn.* gather

cook To use heat to get food ready for eating: We *cooked* the eggs on the stove. **cooked, cooking**

corn A vegetable, often yellow, which has kernels that grow on a cob: We are having *corn* for supper.

cornstalk The stem of a corn plant: We picked the fresh corn right off the *cornstalks.* **cornstalks** ■

costume Special clothes: She was wearing a clown *costume.* **costumes**

covering Something that covers and protects: The bear's fur is a warm *covering.* **coverings** *syns.* shield, overcoat

crayon A stick of colored wax used for drawing and coloring: He used a red *crayon* to color his picture. **crayons** ■

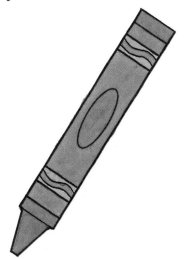

cross To go across or over: They *crossed* over the bridge. **crossed, crossing** *syn.* pass

281

D

darling A person who is loved very much: My *darling* baby brother has a sweet face. **darlings** *syn.* dear

deaf Not able to hear: Mike is *deaf* in one ear.

detective A person who tries to get information to help people solve problems: The *detective* wanted to find out who took the paintings. **detectives** *syn.* private eye

different Not the same or alike: This game is *different* from the one we played before. *syn.* unlike

discover To find out or learn something not known before: We *discovered* a short cut to school. **discovered, discovering** *syns.* find, learn

doll A toy that looks like a person: Her *doll* looks like a real baby. **dolls**

done Finished; through: She is *done* with all her homework. *syns.* finished, through

dough A soft, thick mixture of flour and liquid used for baking things: He made the *dough* for the rolls. ■

dragon A make-believe monster with claws and wings: She read us a story about a castle and a *dragon*. **dragons**

draw To make a picture: Amy will *draw* a cat. **drew, drawing** *syn.* sketch

duckling A baby duck: The *duckling* lives on a farm. **ducklings** ■

E

Earth The planet on which we live, the third planet from the sun: We must keep *Earth* clean. *syn.* world

eat To chew and swallow: I *ate* all my lunch. **ate, eating**

edge The place where something ends: Don't go near the *edge*. **edges** *syn.* rim

electricity Energy that makes light or heat: The lights went off when we lost our *electricity.*

enjoy To have fun: We will *enjoy* the family picnic. **enjoyed, enjoying** *syn.* like

enough As much as needed: Have you seen *enough* animals?

envelope A flat paper wrapper in which a letter is mailed: I will put my letter to Grandma in an *envelope.* **envelopes** ■

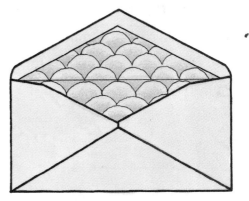

eve The night before: They had a party on New Year's *Eve.* **eves** *syn.* evening

even 1 Besides that: She won the prize for the best runner, and she *even* won the prize for the best jumper! *syn.* also **2** Unlikely as it may seem: He can ride a bike, *even* though no one showed him how. **3** Up to this time: *Even* now, they still write to each other.

ever At any time: Don't *ever* play with matches.

except Other than: Everyone went to the house *except* me.

excuse Pardon: *Excuse* me as I reach across the table. *syn.* pardon

---

F

---

family A person's mother, father, brothers, and sisters: She came back to town to see her *family*. **families** *syns.* relatives, kin

farmer A person who works on a farm: The *farmer* works hard caring for the plants and animals on the farm. **farmers**

farther To a more distant point: She lives *farther* away from school than I do.

favorite A person or thing that is the most liked: This is his *favorite* toy. *syn.* prized

feather The soft covering of a bird: This *feather* is light blue. **feathers** *syn.* down ■

fee Money given to pay for something: He paid a *fee* to use the hall. **fees** *syn.* price

feeler The part of an animal's body used to touch things: The fish uses its *feelers* to find food. **feelers** ▪

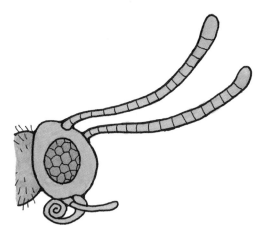

field Land on which plants such as corn and wheat are raised: The farmers worked in the *fields* all day. **fields**

fiesta A party: The most important part of the celebration was the *fiesta*. **fiestas** *syns.* festival, celebration

fifty Forty plus ten, written 50: There are *fifty* people at the party.

fingernail The hard covering at the tip of each finger: Her *fingernails* looked very pretty. **fingernails**

fisherman A person whose job it is to catch fish: The *fisherman* caught fifty fish today. **fishermen** *syn.* angler ▪

forecast A prediction or guess, such as what the weather will be like: Bob listened to the weather *forecast* before he went sailing. **forecasts** *syns.* prediction, guess

285

forward Ahead: They moved *forward* in line.

frame **1** The outside edge of eyeglasses: She wanted glasses with red *frames*. **2** The outside edge of a picture: The *frame* makes the picture look bigger. **frames** ■

fresh New: Harriet loves *freshly* baked bread. **freshly**

fur A covering of thick hair which some animals have: The dog's *fur* keeps it warm.

G

gas Not a solid or a liquid: The rain turned into a *gas* when the weather got warm. **gases**

gerbil A small animal that looks something like a mouse: He took his *gerbil* to school to show everyone. **gerbils** ■

glasses Eyeglasses; something that people wear to help them see better: I can see small letters when I wear my new *glasses*.

gone Not present: All the people are *gone*.

gym A place to play games and work out: He played ball in the *gym* today. **gyms**

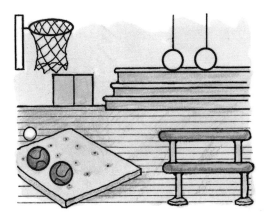

gymnastics Exercises and tricks that use the body's muscles: In *gymnastics*, we learned to do forward rolls.

H

hang To place up above: She *hung* her hat on the hook. **hung, hanging** *syn.* suspend

happy Showing joy: Kate smiled *happily*. **happily** *syns.* cheerful, glad

hearing The ability to experience sound: She has very good *hearing*.

heavy Hard to lift or hold: A car is very *heavy*.

hey A call of surprise or greeting: *Hey*! What's that?

horn A musical instrument that makes loud sounds when blown into: We blew paper *horns* at the birthday party. **horns** ■

hot Having a lot of heat: This room is *hotter* than the library. **hotter, hottest**

hungry Feeling the need to eat: I am *hungry* because I did not finish my lunch. *syn.* starved

hurt 1 To cause pain: Don't *hurt* the dog. *syn.* injure **2** To feel pain: Our legs *hurt* from walking so far. **hurt, hurting** *syn.* ache

---

I

---

ice Water that is frozen: Water turns to *ice* in the freezer.

important Having great value: The teacher told us some *important* facts. *syns.* valuable, major

instrument Tools that help one do a special kind of work: The doctor uses special *instruments*. **instruments** *syn.* tool

itself A thing's own self: The cat couldn't stop *itself* when it smelled the fish.

J

---

join To become a part of: She *joins* many clubs each year. **joined, joining**

K

---

keep To continue: He *kept* asking me to stay. **kept, keeping** *syn.* continue

---

L

---

lantern A kind of light that can be carried: Marnie lit the *lantern* in her hand. **lanterns** *syns.* lamp, light ■

law   A rule that people follow: Everyone should learn the *laws* of the town. **laws** *syn.* rule

librarian   A person who runs a library: The *librarian* helps us pick out books. **librarians**

library   A place where books are kept: He went to the *library* to get a book on forecasting. **libraries**

lightning   A flash of light in the sky that comes with storms: Are you afraid of *lightning*?

liquid   A fluid, like water: Milk is a *liquid*. **liquids** *syn.* fluid

listen   To hear by paying attention: Please *listen* to what I say. **listened, listening** *syn.* heed

loud   Making a strong sound: The radio was playing too *loudly*. **loudly** *syn.* noisy

M

marbles   Small glass balls: The children have many different *marbles*. ■

medicine   Something taken by people or animals to make them well: She took the *medicine* three times a day when she was sick.

midnight   Twelve hours after noon: The new day starts at *midnight*.

milk   A liquid that cows make and people drink: Letty poured some *milk*.

minute   Sixty seconds: Please wait a *minute*. **minutes**

money Change or paper that is made to be used to pay for things: He took *money* to pay for the milk. ■

moth An insect that looks something like a butterfly: Don't let the *moths* into the house. **moths** ■

mountain A very high hill: The people climbed the *mountain*. **mountains**

N

necklace A piece of jewelry worn around the neck: Alice put on her *necklace*. **necklaces** ■

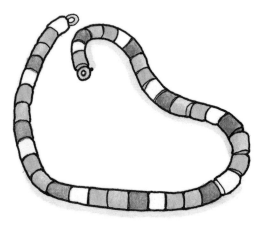

nephew The son of a person's sister or brother: Tony is my *nephew*. **nephews**

nice Pleasant: If you ask *nicely*, most people will be glad to help. **nicely** *syn.* pleasant

nose The part of the body used for smelling and breathing: My *nose* got burned by the sun. **noses**

note A letter that is short: I wrote Emily a *note* to say that I was home. **notes**

notice To see or give attention to: I didn't *notice* you standing there. **noticed, noticing** *syn.* note

---
O
---

often A lot of times: We *often* visit Boston. *syn.* frequently

old Having lived a long time: Sam is *older* than Jeffrey. **older, oldest**

okay All right: *Okay*, I'm ready to go.

once Only one time: I will tell you just *once* what to do.

owner A person who has or owns something: Are you the *owner* of this cat? **owners**

P
---

pair A matching set of two: I have a new *pair* of shoes. **pairs** *syn.* two

pajamas Sleeping clothes: Dina put on her *pajamas*. *syn.* nightwear

parade A line of marchers, often with music: This is a good seat for the *parade*. **parades** ■

parent A mother or father: My *parents* are from Japan. **parents**

party A gathering at which people have fun: My birthday *party* was great. **parties** *syn.* celebration

patch A small piece: There was a *patch* of grass near the tree. **patches** *syn.* plot

picnic An outdoor meal: Let's have a *picnic* in the park today. **picnics** *syn.* cookout

pile A heap of things, one on top of another: There was a *pile* of papers on the desk. **piles** *syns.* heap, stack ■

pillow A soft cushion used for resting the head: I'll fall asleep as soon as I put my head on my *pillow.* **pillows** *syn.* cushion

pitcher A container for liquids: Jerry filled the water *pitcher.* **pitchers** ■

planet A body that moves around the sun: Earth is the *planet* on which we live. **planets**

player A person who plays a sport or game: Lucy is a great baseball *player.* **players**

pocket A small pouch sewn into clothes to put things into: I keep my money in my *pocket.* **pockets** *syn.* pouch

point To show a direction: Which way does the arrow *point*? **pointed, pointing**

pour To make to flow: I *poured* the milk. **poured, pouring**

pretend To make believe: Sam *pretended* that he was a prince. **pretended, pretending.** *syn.* fake

printer A person who makes books or newspapers: I wrote the book and then took it to the *printer.* **printers** ■

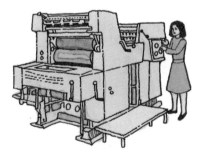

problem Trouble: Our *problem* was that we had nowhere to play. **problems**

promise A sure statement that a person will do something: Kara made a *promise* to me that she would be good. **promises** *syn.* pledge

pupa One part of the life of a butterfly: The caterpillar is called a *pupa* when it is inside its cocoon. **pupas** ■

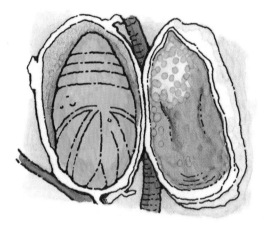

puppy A dog when it is very young: Our *puppy's* name is Sloopy. **puppies** ■

Q

quick Fast: Bring a rag to me *quickly*. **quickly** *syns.* speedy, fast

quiet Not noisy: It is *quiet* by the sea. *syn.* silent

R

really Truly: Are you *really* from Spain? *syn.* truly

remember To bring something back to mind: I *remember* going to Chicago. **remembered, remembering** *syn.* recall

report A telling about something: We read a *report* of the fire in the newspaper. **reports** *syn.* account

rescue Something done to save people or things: Ben came to the *rescue* of the cat. **rescues** *syn.* save

ribbon A thin strip of cloth: Jenny put a *ribbon* in her hair. **ribbons** ■

rough Not even or smooth: The stone felt *rough. syn.* bumpy

S

sailor A person who works on a ship: The *sailors* worked on a large ship. **sailors** ■

294

scare To make frightened: You will *scare* me if you don't knock before you come in. **scared, scaring** *syn.* frighten

seashore Land along the ocean: Boston is on the *seashore. syns.* coast, shore ■

servant A person who works for another, especially in a house: The *servants* brought the king's tea. **servants**

sew To make or fix with thread and needle: Aunt Lil *sewed* Shelly's dress. **sewed, sewing** *syn.* stitch

shadow A dark spot that is seen when light is blocked: When the sun comes up, my *shadow* gets longer. **shadows** ■

signal A sign that means something: We learned the hand *signals* for left and right turns. **signals** *syn.* sign

silver A whitish metal: The *silver* necklace was pretty. ■

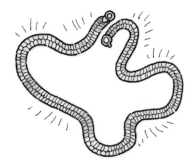

simple Plain; ordinary: We live in a *simple* house by the sea. *syns.* plain, ordinary

sister A woman or girl with the same parents as another person: The Graham *sisters* live there. **sisters**

skates Blades or wheels put on the feet that let the person wearing them move over the ice or roll on a smooth surface: Erica put on her *skates* and headed for the ice. ■

skin A covering on the outside of something: The sun feels warm on my *skin*.

slow Not fast: Speak *slowly*. **slowly**

soft Not hard: The cat's fur is *soft*.

song Sounds made by singing: The *songs* of the people were part of the celebration. **songs** *syns.* tune, melody

speak To talk: I *spoke* to the new girl yesterday. **spoke, speaking** *syn.* talk

spill To come out in a rush: The tears *spilled* out of Matt's eyes. **spilled, spilling** *syn.* overflow ■

splash To splatter with water, mud, or the like: Don't *splash* mud on me! **splashed, splashing** ■

sport An athletic game: Basketball is my favorite *sport.* **sports** *syns.* game, contest

storyteller Someone who tells stories: *Storytellers* help children enjoy themselves. **storytellers** *syn.* narrator

storytelling The art of telling stories: *Storytelling* is a great job.

sudden Happening fast: The rain began *suddenly.* **suddenly**

sunny Bright with the light of the sun: Today it will be *sunny. syn.* bright

super Better than others: Tonia is a *super* math student.

supper The meal eaten in the evening: We'll have popcorn after *supper. syn.* dinner

suppose To require or expect: I'm *supposed* to do my homework before playing. **supposed, supposing** *syn.* expect

---

T

table A kind of furniture with legs and a top: We ate at the *table.* **tables** ■

teacher Someone who helps others learn: Mr. Moltz is a *teacher.* **teachers** *syn.* instructor

thirty-one Thirty plus one: Mike is *thirty-one* years old.

through In one end and out the other: We went *through* the hall to the kitchen.

thunder The loud sound that goes with lightning: The *thunder* scared the dog.

ticket A paper, or card, that means a person can do something or go someplace: I lost my *ticket* to the game. **tickets** ■

tough Hard to cut: The meat was too *tough* to eat.

trip 1 To fall over something: The rock in the path made me *trip.* **tripped, tripping** *syn.* stumble **2** A move from one place to another: He went on a plane *trip.* **trips** *syn.* journey

turkey A large bird: The *turkey* is an ugly bird. **turkeys** ■

U

ugly Awful to look at: The dress was *ugly,* but the coat was even *uglier.* **uglier, ugliest**

unpack To take things out of: We *unpacked* the boxes when we got to our new house. **unpacked, unpacking**

until Till: I will read *until* supper. *syn.* till

V

vegetable A plant used as food: The foods Amy liked best were *vegetables.* **vegetables** ▪

visit 1 To come to see: He can *visit* us every day. **visited, visiting 2** A time when a person comes to see someone else: They came for a short *visit.* **visits**

W

warm Between hot and cold: I love *warm* days for playing outside.

wear To have on: You should be *wearing* a coat. **wore, wearing**

weather What it is like outside: We will go out on the boat when the *weather* is good.

welcome A greeting that means a person is happy that another has come: *Welcome* to the Stanley School.

wheelchair A chair on wheels used by people who cannot walk: Jane used a *wheelchair* when she broke her leg. **wheelchairs** ■

while A time: He will come home in a *while*.

whole All of: I saw the *whole* show. *syn.* entire

wiggle To move from side to side: The puppy *wiggled* as it sat on David's lap. **wiggled, wiggling** *syn.* squirm

window A hole in a wall, usually covered with glass: The *windows* are open so the wind can blow in. **windows**

winter The part of the year that follows fall: There is ice on the pond in *winter.* **winters**

woman A grown-up female person: The two *women* worked together. **women** *syn.* lady

wonder To want to find out about: I *wondered* why Eddie called. **wondered, wondering**

wonderful Very good: That book was *wonderful. syn.* great

wood A forest: Let's walk through the *woods.* **woods** *syn.* forest ■

wooden Made from wood: Children have played with *wooden* toys for many years.

worry To feel uneasy about something: I *worried* when you were late. **worried, worrying** *syn.* fret

write To make up stories and put them down on paper: I would love to *write* for a newspaper. **wrote, writing**

wrong Not right: He turned down the *wrong* road.

Y

yell To speak or make a sound in a loud voice: Martin *yelled* to his sister across the street. **yelled, yelling** *syns.* scream, shout

young Not old: The *young* boy played ball with his mother.

Word List

The following words are introduced in this book. Each is listed beside the number of the page on which it first appears.

Watch Out, Ronald Morgan!
(6–13)

6   glasses
    superkid
    patch
    ice
    yelled
    pile
    hung
    gerbil
7   winter
8   note
    point
9   clear
    frames
    nose
    while
11 wearing
    class
    trip
12 hey

Benjamin Franklin's Glasses
(14–19)

14 printer
    discovered
    electricity
    write

    even
    laws
15 hotter
16 older
    pair
18 bifocals
    kept

Nick Joins In
(20–29)

20 joins
    teacher
    parents
    wheelchair
21 spilled
22 spoke
    because
24 gym
    windows
26 edge
28 excuse
    rescue

Draw Conclusions
(32–33)

32 clues
    given
    paragraph
33 understand
    selection

Jane Martin, Dog Detective
(34–45)

34 detective
    fee
    cents
42 once

Reality and Fantasy
(46–47)

46 reality
    fantasy
    fiction
    realistic
    really
47 decide

Barkley
(48–55)

48 wrong
49 bow
50 hurt
    slowly
    owner
54 young

Dogs at Work
(58–63)

58 deaf
59 listen
60 cross
61 hearing ear
   signals
62 baby

Clyde Monster
(70–77)

70 problem
   uglier
   family
   supposed
74 ever
   scare

Cause and Effect
(80–81)

80 cause
   effect
   reason

Sun Up, Sun Down
(82–87)

82 planet
   Earth
   warm
83 cereal
   whole

Forecast
(88–99)

88 forecast
   party
   weather
   forecaster
89 shadow
   sunny
   lightning
   thunder
92 instruments
97 feather

Maps
(102–105)

103 legend
104 zone
105 remember

Splash
(106–111)

106 splash
107 through
    gas
    becomes
108 mountain
    brook

Owl and the Moon
(112–117)

112 seashore
114 farther
    along
    supper
115 loudly
    gone
    pajamas
116 silver
    pillow

How the Sun Made a Promise and Kept It
(118–127)

118 promise
    beautiful
120 itself
123 enough
124 fur
    rough
    tough

Beatrice Doesn't Want to
(134–143)

134 library
    brother
    report
135 until
136 notice
137 suddenly
138 heavy
    librarian

Main Idea and Details
(144–145)

144 details
    often

Tell Me a Story
(146–151)

146 storytelling
    storytellers
147 circle
148 corn
149 different
150 important visit
    wonderful

The Simple Prince
(152–163)

152 simple
servants
clothes
153 picnic
farmer
156 done
poured
pitcher
157 hungry
butter
158 milk
159 churn
dough
162 nicely
quickly
happily

Jenny and the Tennis Nut
(166–175)

166 minute
170 player
171 sport
enjoy
172 soft
gymnastics
173 belong
174 okay

The Ugly Duckling
(178–185)

178 characters
duckling

179 turkey
alone

The Caterpillar's Surprise
(186–191)

186 caterpillars
moths
187 skin
188 fingernail
crayon
covering
cocoon
pupa
189 body
feelers
wiggles
190 liquid

Follow Directions
(192–195)

192 order
193 ruler
pencil
straight

Grandma Without Me
(202–209)

204 darling
208 draw

Summarize
(212–213)

212 summarize
summary

Scrapbooks
(214–219)

215 collects
favorite
217 ticket

The Year of the Smile
(220–229)

220 celebration
envelope
money
221 ribbon
lantern
puppy's
224 doll
costume
parade
225 table
scissors
226 dragon
227 forward

New Year's Day
(230–235)

230 celebrate
231 eve
midnighty
horns
cities
232 songs
fiesta
234 city

Story Elements
(238–239)

238 elements
   solution

Cornstalks and Cannonballs
(240–251)

240 cornstalks
   cannonballs
241 fishermen
   fields
   cannons
242 worried
   wondered
243 sailors
   vegetables

244 angry
249 women

The Quilt Story
(252–259)

252 sewed
253 quiet
   woods
   pretended
   sisters
254 built
   wooden
   welcome
255 except
   attic
258 freshly
   unpacked

Arthur's Honey Bear
(260–273)

260 buys
261 marbles
262 medicine
263 thirty-one
264 arrows
266 fifty
   pocket
267 none
268 broken
269 necklace
272 nephews

8
D 9
E 0
F 1
G 2
H 3
I 4
J 5